The Easter Rising
Revolution and
Irish Nationalism

AHM Europe Since 1500 Series

The Easter Rising
Revolution and Irish Nationalism

Alan J. Ward
The College of William and Mary

AHM Publishing Corporation
Arlington Heights, Illinois 60004

PRINTED IN THE UNITED STATES OF AMERICA
7129

Preface

The political and military crisis which has engulfed Northern Ireland for more than ten years has had at least one beneficial effect. It has provoked some serious rethinking about the course of Irish history. Old interpretations of Ireland's past may have contributed to the present agony, and it may be that fresh inquiries into the origins of this apparently insoluble problem will help in the search for its solution. It is a truism that the way we write and teach about the past is as influential as the events of the past themselves, and it is extremely important, therefore, that we reconsider the historical record from time to time.

This book attempts such a reconsideration by examining the most dramatic event in modern Irish history, the Easter Rising of 1916, to ask why it occurred and what its influence has been. There are several reasons for focussing on this one event. First, the Rising is important in its own right; it changed the course of Irish history. Second, the Rising provides us with a criterion for selection to explore some important themes in Irish history without pretending to be engaged in a comprehensive history. Third, and most important, the Rising is at the heart of a controversy revived by the present crisis in Northern Ireland. That controversy concerns no less than the value of the Easter Rising and the revolutionary tradition. There are those, for example, who now argue that the Rising was unnecessary and spawned a tradition of violence which has bedevilled Irish political and social development.

I drew heavily from my own research in Irish politics and history, both published and unpublished, for this study and from the substantial literature which already exists on this subject, much of which I acknowledge in the biblography. However, I also drew upon the advice I have received through the years from a large number of friends and colleagues in the field of Irish studies in the United States. These include particularly the historians Lawrence McCaffrey, Thomas Hachey and Joseph Curran, who have given generously of both time and hospitality. They may disagree with portions of this book, but I am grateful nonetheless. I am also heavily indebted to Martha Stanley for her enormous help in preparing the manuscript.

For convenience, and to correspond with common usage, the name Ireland is used in this book interchangeably with Irish Free State, Eire, and Republic of Ireland when dealing with the period since partition in 1921. Northern Ireland refers to the six counties which separated from the rest of Ireland in 1921.

Alan Ward

CONTENTS

IRELAND

★ Capitols
● County Towns
〰 Country Boundary
〜 Gaelic Provinces
〜 Counties

Part I. The Event

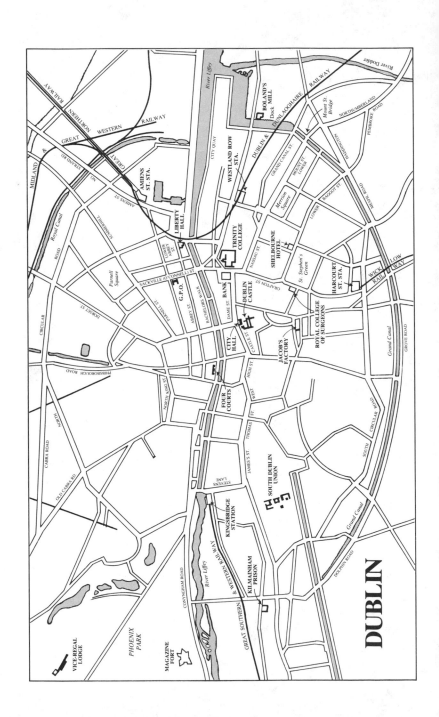

DUBLIN

1

The Easter Rising

This is a book about the causes and effects of the 1916 Easter Rising in Dublin. First, however, we have to know something about the Rising itself. What actually happened in Dublin that week?

April 24, 1916, was Easter Monday and Dubliners were enjoying a public holiday. Many had left the city for the Fairyhouse races, and others were visiting the Royal Dublin Society Show. The weather was fine and the atmosphere relaxed when, at midday, peace was shattered by a rebellion in the city. Six days later portions of Dublin lay in ruins, hundreds were homeless, factories and shops were closed, one hundred thousand people—a third of the population—were on public relief, hundreds had died, and thousands were wounded.

The leaders of this rebellion might easily have been arrested long before it occurred. They had been conducting a campaign against British army recruiting in Ireland since World War I began in 1914, with antiwar newspapers, pamphlets, posters and demonstrations. Irishmen, they insisted, should not fight for the freedom of others until Ireland itself was free. Those who participated in the rebellion had openly been drilling and parading in Ireland with rifles and other weapons.

The overt dissidents were a small minority in a country which had supplied thousands of volunteers for the army, but the government treated them with considerable caution. Some antiwar activists were deported to Britain and seditious newspapers were banned, but the minister responsible for Ireland, Chief Secretary Augustine Birrell, opposed any systematic suppression of the movement. He feared that it would precipitate an Irish crisis which would weaken the overall war effort. For this reason Ireland was excluded from conscription when it was introduced into the United Kingdom in January 1916. Irishmen could argue that they were serving a higher Irish patriotism by refusing to be conscripted to fight for England, and their protests might arouse the latent antipathy to England which had always existed in Ireland. The government concluded that, so long as Ireland supplied volunteers for the army and food for industrial Britain, and so long as the antiwar dissidents were few in number, there would be no conscription and little repression.

By Easter 1916, however, the dissidents, known by the government and the general public as Sinn Feiners, had gone too far. Rumors had flourished in Dublin for some time that a rebellion was planned, and two events on Easter Saturday confirmed this suspicion. First, the navy captured a disguised German merchant ship carrying weapons and ammunition to the rebels. Its captain scuttled the ship at Queenstown, now known as Cobh, outside Cork. Second, Sir Roger Casement, a retired British diplomat–turned–Irish–revolutionary who had been recruiting a brigade to fight against England from Irish prisoners of war in Germany, was captured from a German submarine soon after landing in Tralee Bay. The government immediately assumed that these events signified a treasonous conspiracy between the Irish rebels and Britain's enemy, Germany.

A German conspiracy was clearly intolerable, and Lord Wimborne, the lord lieutenant of Ireland, and Sir Matthew Nathan, the under secretary and head of the Irish administration, cabled Birrell in London for permission to arrest the Sinn Fein leaders. They were too late. Nathan was in Dublin Castle, headquarters of the Irish administration, planning the arrests and awaiting permission to move, when the first shots were fired in the Easter Rising and the Castle itself came under fire.

Despite the concern of Wimborne and Nathan, Dublin was totally unprepared for what happened that morning. The holiday was a completely normal one, and General Friend, the British commander in chief in Ireland, was in London on leave. Of the twenty–four hundred soldiers stationed in the city, only four hundred were on duty when at midday the commander in chief of the Irish republican forces, Patrick Pearse, and his deputy, James Connolly, led their troops into action from Liberty Hall, the Irish Transport and General Workers' Union headquarters just north of the River Liffey in central Dublin. Simultaneously, other republicans moved to prearranged sites around Dublin. One small group overpowered the single sentry on duty outside and the eleven men stationed inside the Phoenix Park Magazine Fort. This group carried away some arms and ammunition and blew up a small arms store, but they could not destroy the main store because the officer in charge had taken the key with him to the races! As a result, the great explosion meant to signal the beginning of the Rising was only a whimper.

The republican army was an absurdly small group for such an enterprise. The original plans for the Rising called for up to five thousand men to move in Dublin and thousands more throughout the country, perhaps as many as ten thousand in all. The leaders had hoped for German arms and even a German expeditionary force, but the Germans sent no men and their weapons were sunk in the waters off Queenstown. Futhermore, because of a leadership dispute, only about eight hundred obeyed the order to assemble in Dublin on Easter Monday. Others joined in during the week, but it is unlikely that more than fifteen hundred armed republicans were involved in all. They were supported by cooks and nurses from the Cumann na mBan, a republican women's organization, and by messengers from Fianna Eireann, a republican boy scout organization. But in everyone of the locations they occupied, the republicans mustered only about one fourth of their anticipated strength. Nevertheless, the Rising lasted six days. The famous rebellion of 1803, led by Robert Emmet, had lasted only one evening.

The republicans presented a rather incongruous sight. Some wore the uniforms of an organization known as the Irish Volunteers and others the uniforms of the two–hundred–man Irish Citizen Army, the militia of the Irish Transport and General Workers' Union. The majority wore only belts or military equipment over their civilian clothes. Their weapons were even more diverse than their garb. One author described them: "The resistive appliances unwrapped on that Monday morning were a quartermaster's nightmare. . . . The rifles started with Sniders from old God's time and formed a chronology of arms–through–the–ages."[1] Shotguns, rifles and pistols of every gauge, grenades, homemade bombs, pikes and spears went out to face the British army.

In 1803, Emmet had planned to capture Dublin Castle. The 1916 republicans could easily have accomplished this because the small group that attacked the castle at about noon found only one policeman on duty at the gate, whom they killed, and six soldiers in the guard room, whom they surprised and overpowered. Another twenty–five soldiers were in the castle garrison nearby, but none stood between the attackers and Sir Matthew Nathan in the main body of the castle. Had the attacking force been at full strength, or had they even anticipated such a light guard, both Dublin Castle and the undersecretary could have been seized in the opening minutes of the Rising. Instead, the rebels retreated to surrounding buildings, including the Dublin City Hall, from which they were flushed out by army fire on Tuesday.

The capture of the castle was just one example of the ease with which major buildings in the city could be taken. The Phoenix Park Magazine Fort was captured with ease. The First Battalion of the Dublin brigade of the republican forces, under Commandant Edward Daly, quickly occupied the Four Courts, home of the Irish judiciary, on the north bank of the River Liffey in the heart

[1] Redmond Fitzgerald, *Cry Blood, Cry Erin* (New York, 1966), p.75.

of the city. Although surrounding buildings and streets, particularly North King Street, were the scene of savage fighting, the Four Courts were held by the rebels until they surrendered the following Saturday. To the west of the inner city, the South Dublin Union, a fifty–two acre workhouse, and some surrounding buildings were held by 120 men of the Fourth Battalion under Commandant Eamonn Ceannt. Despite heavy fighting at close quarters, these were held until Sunday.

The bulk of the Irish Citizen Army, under Commandant Michael Mallin and his second–in–command, Countess Constance Markiewicz, the Irish wife of a Polish count, occupied St. Stephen's Green, a large square south of the Liffey. They came under heavy British machine gun fire on Tuesday morning from the Shelbourne Hotel, north of the square and were forced to retreat to the College of Surgeons, to the west of the square. There they were able to hold out, though very short of food, until Sunday. A little to the west of St. Stephen's Green was Jacob's Biscuit Factory, a stronghold which saw no major fighting and which was occupied until Sunday by 150 men of the Second Battalion under Commandant Thomas MacDonagh. To the east of the central city, 130 men of the Third Battalion under Commandant Eamon de Valera occupied Boland's Flour Mill, and these, too, surrendered on Sunday.

The heaviest fighting of the Rising occurred at the Mount Street Bridge where seventeen republicans occupied Clanwilliam House and other buildings covering a bridge over the Grand Canal. This was the route taken into Dublin on Wednesday morning by a thousand British reinforcements who had landed at Kingstown (now Dun Laoghaire), six miles south of Dublin, the previous night. Over two hundred soldiers were killed or wounded before the handful of surviving republicans was forced to retreat under machine gun fire and overwhelming numbers.

Mount Street Bridge and North King Street, near the Four Courts, saw the heaviest battles of the Rising, and there was heavy fighting both at the South Dublin Union and around Dublin Castle, but the symbolic heart of the Rising was the General Post Office

(G.P.O.) building on what was then known as Sackville Street, the main street in Dublin. The street runs north of the O'Connell Bridge on the Liffey and is now O'Connell Street. When Pearse and Connolly left Liberty Hall at midday on Easter Monday, they marched with approximately one hundred and fifty volunteers to the G.P.O. a short distance away. They stormed into the building and overpowered the unarmed guard of seven. Shortly afterwards, Pearse reappeared on the steps to read the Proclamation of the Irish Republic.

THE PROCLAMATION OF THE IRISH
REPUBLIC (1916)

Poblacht na h–Eireann
The Provisional Government
of the
IRISH REPUBLIC
To the people of Ireland

Irishmen and Irishwomen: In the name of God and of the dead generations from which she receives her old tradition of nationhood, Ireland, through us, summons her children to her flag and strikes for her freedom.

Having organised and trained her manhood through her secret revolutionary organisation, the Irish Republican Brotherhood, and through her open military organizations, the Irish Volunteers and the Irish Citizen Army, having patiently perfected her discipline, having resolutely waited for the right moment to reveal itself, she now seizes that moment, and, supported by her exiled children in America and by gallant allies in Europe, but relying in the first on her own strength, she strikes in full confidence of victory.

We declare the right of the people of Ireland to the ownership of Ireland, and to the unfettered control of Irish destinies, to be sovereign and indefeasible. The long usurpation of that right by a foreign people and government has not extinguished the right, nor can it ever be extinguished except by the destruction of the Irish people. In every generation the Irish people have asserted their right to national freedom and sovereignty; six times during the past three hundred years they have asserted it in arms. Standing on that fundamental right and again asserting it in arms in the face of the world, we hereby proclaim the Irish Republic as a Sovereign Independent State, and we pledge our lives and the lives of our comrades-in-arms to the cause of its freedom, of its welfare, and of its exaltation among the nations. The Irish Republic is entitled to, and hereby claims, the allegiance of every Irishman and Irishwoman. The Republic guarantees religious and civil liberty, equal rights and equal opportunities to all its citizens, and declares its resolve to pursue the happiness and prosperity of the whole nation and of all its parts, cherishing all the children of the nation equally, and oblivious of the differences carefully fostered by an alien government, which have divided a minority from the majority in the past.

Until our arms have brought the opportune moment for the establishment of a permanent National Government, representative of the whole people of Ireland, and elected by the suffrages of all her men and women, the Provisional Government, hereby constituted, will administer the civil and military affairs of the Republic in trust for the people.

We place the cause of the Irish Republic under the protection of the Most High God, Whose blessing we invoke upon our arms, and we pray that no one who serves that cause will dishonour it by cowardice, inhumanity or rapine. In this supreme hour the Irish nation must, by its valour and discipline and by the readiness of its children to sacrifice themselves for the common good, prove itself worthy of the august destiny to which it is called.

Signed on Behalf of the Provisional Government,

THOMAS J. CLARKE

SEAN MACDIARMADA   THOMAS MACDONAGH
P. H. PEARSE   EAMONN CEANNT
JAMES CONNOLLY   JOSEPH PLUNKETT

Pearse, Connolly, Clarke, Plunkett and MacDiarmada all fought at the G.P.O. Ceannt lead the forces at the South Dublin Union and MacDonagh those at Jacob's Biscuit Factory.[2] All seven lived through Easter week but eventually were to pay for their audacity with their lives.

[2] Sean MacDiarmada's English name was John MacDermott. Ceannt was known as Edward Kent.

Having called the Irish Republic into existence, Pearse, its president and commander in chief, returned to the G.P.O, home of the provisional government; and the flag of the Republic was hoisted over the building, where it remained for six days.

Pearse and his colleagues did not expect to defeat the army, for how could they? As James Connolly left Liberty Hall, he confessed to a friend, "We're going out to be slaughtered, you know."[3] But he went because, he, Pearse, and the other leaders believed that only a heroic gesture, a blood sacrifice, an act of voluntary martyrdom, could reawaken Republican Nationalism in Ireland. MacDiarmada wrote from his cell in Kilmainham Prison on the eve of his execution, "We die that the Irish nation may live. Our blood will rebaptise and reinvigorate the land."[4]

In the early months of the war, a sign on Liberty Hall had read, "We serve neither King nor Kaiser, but Ireland," and all the evidence now available indicates this to have been true. At the time, however, the government, and perhaps a majority of Irishmen, saw things very differently. The reference to "gallant allies in Europe" in the Proclamation of the Irish Republic had been a rhetorical flourish, but Lord Wimborne's proclamation on Easter Monday spoke of "an attempt, instigated and designated by the foreign enemies of our king and country."[5] The London *Times* spoke of "a carefully-arranged plot, concocted between the Irish traitors and their German confederates."[6] John Redmond, the leader of the Irish Nationalists in Parliament since 1900, accused the rebels of insanely destroying forty years of progress towards self-government. Of the Rising, he said on April 28, "Germany plotted it, Germany organized it, Germany paid for it."[7] The government believed that zeppelin attacks on London and the shelling of English east coast ports by German warships had been

---

[3] Fitzgerald, p. 79.
[4] Fitzgerald, p. 109.
[5] Charles Duff, *Six Days to Shake an Empire* (New York, 1966), p. 121.
[6] London *Times*, 26 April 1916.
[7] London *Times*, 29 April 1916.

coordinated with the Rising to divert military attention from the event in Ireland.

To the government, then, this was not simply an Irish rebellion, which would have been bad enough in the middle of a great war. It was a German plot which had to be crushed. The government moved quickly to bring in troop reinforcements, artillery, armored cars and even a gunboat which began to operate on the River Liffey on Wednesday. By 4:00 P.M. on Monday, reinforcements began to arrive in Dublin from the barracks at the Curragh in County Kildare, southwest of Dublin. By early Tuesday morning there were 4,650 soldiers from Ireland in Dublin and more were to come. Martial law was proclaimed for Dublin that evening and for the whole of Ireland the following day. Reinforcements from England began to arrive in the city on Wednesday, the day Sir John Maxwell was assigned to command the operation. By the end of the week, about 12,000 in government troops were ranged against the republicans.

The government acted decisively, but cautiously. Throughout the week, it lacked information concerning the strength of the republicans and, for a short while, feared both a general uprising in the country and a German invasion. The military plan in Dublin was to overwhelm the republicans with artillery and superior numbers over a period of days. Beginning on Tuesday, the army isolated the republican strongholds from each other, occupied a line just south of the River Liffey from Kingsbridge Station in the west to Trinity College in the east, cordoned off the inner city north of the river and placed two smaller cordons around the Four Courts and the G.P.O.

With the exception of the battle for Mount Street Bridge and a sixteen hour battle at North King Street, there were no major engagements between the two forces. The republicans were well entrenched and attempts to storm their positions would have meant heavy government casualties, as happened unnecessarily at Mount Street Bridge on Wednesday afternoon when the army could have retreated and used other routes to the city. The G.P.O.

was shelled by artillery, machine gun and rifle fire for five days from a considerable distance, but no attempt was made to assault it. Republicans occupied the major buildings for about one hundred yards around the G.P.O. virtually until the surrender, finally yielding not to an attack but to a raging fire. Incendiary shells from government artillery set fire to buildings in Abbey Street on Thursday morning. The fire spread to Sackville Street, and at 4:00 P.M. on Friday the G.P.O. itself was hit and fired. By 7:00 P.M. the building had to be evacuated. The leaders of the Rising—Pearse, Clarke, Plunkett, MacDermott and Connolly, the latter crippled by a bullet wound he received in the street on Thursday—spent their last night of freedom in a small house on Moore Street, just behind the G.P.O.

By Friday evening, the republicans had taken considerable casualties from four days of almost continuous artillery and rifle fire, and Sackville Street and its surroundings had been devastated. But there had been no decisive battle. Some of the republican positions—Jacob's Biscuit Factory and Boland's Mill, for example—had seen relatively little action. Nevertheless, on Saturday Pearse and Connolly decided to surrender. They had been forced out of the G.P.O. and were surrounded. An attempt to link with their colleagues in the Four Courts was impossible because of the cordon. Their men had been contained for four days in a shell–shocked building, casualties had been heavy and supplies were short. Furthermore, Dublin had suffered terribly. Parts of the city were devasted by artillery and fire. Hundreds had been trapped in their homes by the vicious crossfire of snipers hidden in buildings and behind street barricades, and many innocent people had been killed by stray bullets. The republicans had made their point, and the G.P.O. headquarters group was ready to surrender. Pearse knew that death awaited him no matter what the immediate outcome of the Rising, and on Friday morning, knowing the end was near, he prepared a statement for his troops which said, "I am satisfied that we have saved Ireland's honour."[8]

At 12:45 P.M. on Saturday, Nurse Elizabeth O'Farrell, who had been in the G.P.O. from the beginning, left Moore Street under cover of a white flag to announce that Pearse was ready to discuss a surrender. She was told that the surrender had to be unconditional. At 2:30 P.M. Pearse himself accompanied Miss O'Farrell. He was taken to General Maxwell and signed his general surrender order at 3:45 P.M. It was later cosigned by Connolly and Thomas Mac-Donagh. Nurse O'Farrell and a British officer carried the orders to each of the republican positions around the city, finishing on Sunday. Only the G.P.O. had been lost of all the major sites occupied in strength on Monday. Hundreds of republicans had survived at the Four Courts, the South Dublin Union, Jacob's Biscuit Factory, the College of Surgeons and Boland's Mill, and many of them felt that the Rising should continue, but the surrender order was finally accepted. The remnants of the republican army were taken into custody and marched through a shocked and relieved city on Sunday morning.

The Rising, in its most immediate sense, was over, although firing could still be heard on Tuesday. Precise casualty figures are difficult to obtain, but, in the official reckoning, about four hundred and fifty people had died, and twenty–five hundred were wounded.[9] The republican and civilian dead were difficult to distinguish from each other but it was estimated that over sixty rebels had died. The republicans were certainly not received as heroes. The country had not risen in their support, and the Irish Nationalists in Parliament had condemned them. Outside Dublin, support for the Rising had been miniscule. Republicans had captured some positions in County Galway, County Wexford, and County Louth, but no major city or town had staged its own rising.

The population of Dublin, where normal life had ceased on

[8] Max Caulfield, *The Easter Rebellion* (London, 1965), p. 309.
[9] Great Britain, *Documents Relative to the Sinn Fein Movement*, Cmd. 1108, xxix, 429, 1921, pp. 14–15.

Easter Monday, had been more than simply inconvenienced. Many had paid with their lives. In the cordoned inner city, food supplies had run out and elsewhere in the city they were seriously disrupted. Gas supplies for cooking and light had been cut for most of the city on Monday. Soon banks and many work places and shops were closed, and public transport and postal services ceased. The inner city housed some of the worst slums in Europe, and the slum poor looted much of Sackville Street in the first days of the Rising. At another point on the social scale, the middle class regarded the Rising with horror. Redmond Fitzgerald described these feelings:

> The insurection had not carried the people with it. The crowds who poured out of the tenements did not feel at one with these grim young men who gave them orders and pushed them back from the shops that lay bursting with things they had coveted all their pinched lives. It did not carry the lace–curtain Irish with it either, for respectable lives were being disrupted and you dare not go the grocers. So the two Dublins, who hated each other, united in contempt for these upstarts and their Republic.[10]

The Easter Rising was not a popular rebellion, not on Sunday, April 30, when Dubliners inspected a scene in central Dublin reminiscent of newspaper photographs of war–shattered towns in France and Belgium. But, though few yet realized it, the Rising had accomplished a great deal. One who recognized this was the writer James Stephens, who had already completed an eye–witness account for publication by May 6. He wrote, "[Ireland] was not with the revolution, but in a few months she will be, and her heart which was withering will be warmed by the knowledge that men have thought her worth dying for."[11] Another who quickly came to understand was W. B. Yeats, who was in England during the Rising but described his feelings in the poem, *Easter 1916*, com-

[10] Fitzgerald, p. 88.
[11] James Stephens, *The Insurrection in Dublin* (Dublin, 1966) p. 8.

posed in September of that year. He had not liked or been impressed by the leaders of the Rising as he had known them in the past. He was polite to them, the poets Pearse and MacDonagh, for example, but condescending. Of Constance Markiewicz, he wrote:

> That woman's days were spent
> In ignorant good–will
> Her nights in arguments
> Until her voice grew shrill.

He thought John MacBride, who was executed on May 5, "A drunken, vainglorious lout." But, Yeats confessed:

> He, too, has been changed in his turn,
> Transformed utterly:

In his final stanza, Yeats paid tribute to the Rising:

> And what if excess of love
> Bewildered them till they died?
> I write it out in verse—
> MacDonagh and MacBride
> And Connolly and Pearse
> Now and in time to be,
> Wherever green is worn,
> Are changed, changed utterly:
> A terrible beauty is born.[12]

[12] J. B. Yeats, *Collected Poems* (London, 1958), pp. 202–205.

Part II. "Why Did It Happen?"

2
England and Ireland

What was it that led these few into rebellion when most Irish men and women believed the United Kingdom was fighting a just war in Europe? The reasons are complex, and to understand them we have to start at the beginning. We have to know something about the stormy history of Anglo–Irish relations. The Easter Rising was not inevitable, but it was a natural consequence of the conflicts of the past.

THE CONQUEST OF IRELAND

In approximately 1155, Pope Adrian IV, who was born in England, granted the lordship of Ireland to the king of England, Henry II, in his Bull *Laudabiliter*.[1] Irish nationalists subsequently charged that the only English pope in the history of the Church authorized the English conquest of Ireland, an accusation that can still be heard occasionally in Ireland. It misrepresents what happened in several ways. Adrian was not an English imperialist. His intention was to bring order to Ireland and to bring the Irish Church more firmly under the control of Rome. Furthermore, Henry II was Norman, not English. The Normans had invaded England in 1066,

[1] Edmund Curtis and R. B. McDowell, eds., *Irish Historical Documents, 1172–1922* (New York, 1968), p. 17.

and the English nation which we know today had not been defined in the twelfth century.

When the Normans actually went to Ireland in 1169, it was as adventurers, not imperialists. Furthermore, it was at the invitation of an Irish king, Dermot MacMurrough, who recruited a small number of Normans and Welsh to assist him in recovering the throne of Leinster, one of many kingdoms in Ireland. A much larger force, under the earl of Pembroke, known as Strongbow, landed in 1170. Strongbow married the daughter of Dermot and secured the throne of Leinster on the death of the king. It was to check the growth of what he feared might be a rival Norman state in Ireland that Henry II landed in Ireland in 1171. He confirmed Strongbow's claim to Leinster in return for a pledge of loyalty to the crown and received the homage of other kings in Ireland. Henry held court in Dublin for some months, but his presence in Ireland fell far short of conquest. The Normans did not conquer Ireland as they had conquered England. Henry was lord of Ireland in name only, and the country continued to be governed by kings and chiefs, who were either native Irish or, following Strongbow's example, Normans. For centuries Ireland remained what it had been before the Normans came, an arena for local rivalries and wars. It was not governed from England in any real sense and was too torn by internecine warfare to govern itself as a single state.

The kings of England sought to manage Ireland through a feudal pact between the crown and the many Irish kings and chiefs. The system failed because the crown could not physically control the rivalries and ambitions of the local rulers, many of whom were native Irish with no appreciation of feudal allegiance. The Norman settlers were themselves too far from the throne to be easily managed, and many were transformed into a new class by intermarriage with the native Irish. The Statutes of Kilkenny in 1366 were designed to prevent this dilution by intermarriage of the settler stock. In the eastern and central parts of Ireland, settlers were forbidden to adopt the Irish language and culture, and the native Irish were required to adopt English ways. The rest of the country was to be abandoned to the native Irish. This policy failed, but it recognized that there were two Irelands. There was an English or settlers' Ireland and a Gaelic Ireland. The crown actually possessed only nominal control of the anglicized portion of the country, where the Statutes of Kilkenny were not rigidly enforced, but into this area law, government and feudal forms of social organization were imported from England. For example, an Irish Exchequer was created in 1200, the Magna Carta was extended into this part of Ireland in 1217, and an Irish Parliament, with upper and lower houses on the English model, was established in Dublin before the end of the thirteenth century. Gaelic Ireland never developed the indigenous legal and political institutions which might have formed the foundations of a united Ireland. Rather, as Professor J. C. Beckett argues, "The very notion of an Irish state with an effective central government is part of Ireland's English heritage."[2]

The Irish Parliament was never strong. It sat very infrequently—only three times during the reign of Elizabeth I, for example—and its power was limited by Poyning's Law of 1494, which specified that all bills had to be presented to the King and Council in England for approval before their consideration in Ireland. By the late seventeenth century, the Irish Parliament was initiating bills itself, but these still required the English government's approval before passage and this relationship continued until 1782. Furthermore, in the Declaratory Act of 1720, the British Parliament asserted its right to legislate for Ireland. Nevertheless, the notion that Ireland was a separate political community was nourished through the years by this Irish Parliament, albeit the parliament of only the Anglicized portion of the country. Furthermore, although the bulk of the settlers from England supported the imported cultural, social, political and legal forms, they came to see themselves as a distinct class, not English but the English of Ireland.

[2] J. C. Beckett, *The Anglo-Irish Tradition* (London, 1976), p. 22.

It was the Tudors, particularly Henry VIII (1509–1547) and Elizabeth I (1558–1603), who finally brought about the English conquest of Ireland, although they never extinguished the sense that Ireland was a separate political community. By then the reformation had added a new dimension to Anglo–Irish relations because the great majority of the Irish, whether of native or settler stock, remained Catholic and Ireland became an important target for England's Catholic enemy, Spain. Henry II had feared a rival Norman state in Ireland, but the Tudors feared its control by Catholic Spain. The papal Bull *Laudabiliter* of 1154 assigned Ireland to Henry II of England, but the Bull *Rex Hiberniae* of 1555 assigned it to Philip II and Mary of Spain.[3]

By the early sixteenth century, the zone of even nominal royal control in Ireland had been reduced to a fifty–by–twenty mile area around Dublin, the so–called Pale. Even there the earls of Kildare had ruled virtually independently as the kings' deputies for several generations. The greater part of the country was still ruled by the native Irish or the Old English, descendents of the Norman settlers. Ireland was a country of political instability, negligible urban development, and primitive agriculture, with virtually no contact with the broader cultural life of Europe. It was regarded in England as a wild and savage place on the edge of the world. In Elizabethan times, for example, it was thought of as territory like Virginia, ripe for settlement by agents of London companies. Henry VIII moved to change at least the political facts of Ireland.

In 1534, the earl of Kildare was exiled to England, where he died in prison, and his five sons were subsequently executed for rebellion. The power of the Kildares was, therefore, broken in the Pale which was brought firmly under the control of the crown. In 1536 and 1537, the Irish Parliament recognized the supremacy of Henry VIII over the Church in Ireland. At first the Irish bishops accepted this, but they were soon alienated by the dissolution and and confiscation of the monasteries, and the Reformation never

[3] Patrick O'Farrell, *Ireland's English Question: Anglo–Irish Relations, 1534–1970* (London, 1971), p. 20.

came to Ireland. Resistance to English authority, by both the native Irish and the Catholic Old English, came to be linked inextricably to the Roman Catholic Church in Ireland whose power and authority were challenged by England for more than three hundred years.

Henry next attempted to strengthen his hold on the country through the policy of surrender and regrant. All the chiefs and kings of Ireland were required to surrender their land to the crown which then regranted it to them under the feudal relationship of knight service. They were required to abandon Irish names and customs. They could maintain armed forces only with the consent of the crown, and their land would be forfeited if they rebelled. The policy confirmed the titles of the Old English, who already held their land in a feudal relationship to the crown, but it attacked the traditional Irish land tenure system in which land was the property of the tribe rather than the chief. Finally, in 1541 the Irish Parliament recognized Henry VIII as king of Ireland rather than lord, the title dating from the time of Henry II.

These policies—the assertion of the king's supremacy over the Irish Church, surrender and regrant, and the new title of king of Ireland—did not pacify the country nor did they effectively extend the crown's authority beyond the Pale. But they alienated many of the native Irish, the Catholic Old English and the Church. For the remainder of the Tudor period, England feared an alliance between Spain and rebellious Irish because the crown still lacked the physical means to enforce its will in Ireland. It was left to Elizabeth I to bring about the final conquest of Ireland by applying the force which had always been absent before.

Elizabeth reasserted the authority of the crown in Church and state in Ireland with the Acts of Uniformity and Supremacy in 1560, but she did not make the mistake of rigidly enforcing the law. There were areas which remained almost purely Gaelic, as well as Catholic, notably Ulster in the north. The central administration in Dublin was placed in the hands of new Protestant settlers, but the Catholic Old English dominated commerce and the law. Furthermore, when Ireland was divided into counties, Catholics predominated in local administration. Refusing to swear an oath recognizing the religious supremacy of the crown was not an absolute barrier to political or judicial office under the Tudors, who were more concerned with the loyalty of a subject than with his religion. This prudent policy meant that Elizabeth retained the loyalty of most of the Old English Catholics during her reign despite three major Irish rebellions and military intervention from Spain. In 1601, for example, four thousand Spanish troops landed in Kinsale.

Elizabeth was engaged in almost continuous efforts to subdue Ireland, and it was not until Mountjoy was sent to Ireland in 1600 and brutally broke the rebellion of Hugh O'Neill, earl of Tyrone, and Hugh Roe O'Donnell, earl of Tyreconnell, in Ulster, that England—now indisputably English—was able to complete the conquest that the Normans had begun in 1169. The war was won just days after Elizabeth's death in 1603.

The conquest was complete, but the seeds had been sown for the discord to come. The failure of the Reformation and the resiliency of the Irish culture meant that while England could now enforce its military and political authority in Ireland, it could never enforce its spiritual or moral authority. Very little effort was made to convert the Irish either from Roman Catholicism or from the Gaelic culture. Acts of Parliament were passed, from the Statutes of Kilkenny to the Elizabethan Acts of Uniformity and Supremacy, but conversion was not practiced. Catholicism joined the Catholic Old English and native Irish communities together and, despite the gradual spread of the English language and customs, the Gaelic culture persisted among the native Irish, the majority of the population. These two identities, one Catholic and the other native Irish, segregated the great majority in Ireland from the Protestant minority in the population.

THE PLANTATIONS AND THE CROMWELLITE CONFISCATIONS

The Protestant population of Ireland was extremely small until the seventeenth–century policy of plantation, that is, the large–scale settlement of "loyal" English or Scottish immigrants in Ireland. The Catholic Queen Mary (1553–1558) attempted plantations on a small scale, as did Elizabeth, but without success. Ireland had not yet been militarily subdued, and there was an insufficient supply of settlers. Settlement only succeeded during the reign of Elizabeth's successor, James I (1603–1625). It was assisted by the so–called flight of the earls in 1607, when the great lords—the earls of Tyrone and Tyreconnell—and approximately one hundred chiefs left Ulster, the most Gaelic of the Irish provinces. Their lands in six of the nine Ulster counties were declared forfeited and were assigned to undertakers who agreed to lease them to English or Scottish settlers. Derry City, for example, was awarded to the City of London in 1610 and was renamed Londonderry.

In this way, a new class of settlers, largely Scottish and Presbyterian, came to Ulster. Unlike their Norman predecessors, they did not intermarry or adopt Irish customs and always remained apart from the Catholic Irish. Those Catholics who did manage to acquire or retain farms in Ulster settled only the poorest land, and there began the economic, social, and religious segregation that has characterized Ulster ever since. There also began that sense of outrage, of colonial exploitation and oppression that still influences Catholics in Northern Ireland. They are the dispossessed. The contemporary problem of Northern Ireland has its origins, therefore, in the seventeenth–century settlement.

The success of the Ulster plantation led to others, though smaller, in Wexford, Longford, Leitrim, and Connaught. By 1641 approximately forty percent of the land was owned by Protestants and approximately two hundred thousand English and one hundred thirty thousand Scottish Presbyterian settlers had come to Ireland. They were not solely in the North, but the scale of the Ulster plantation was unparalleled, as was its effect on relations between the Catholic and Protestant communities.

Under James I the laws against Catholicism were not repealed, but neither were they strictly enforced for fear of provoking new and costly rebellions. It was only with considerable difficulty, and by creating new boroughs, that the Irish administration was able to secure a Protestant majority in the Irish Parliament, and there were times when the Catholic and Protestant elites made common cause against the crown's demands for subsidies. Indeed, it was a combination of Protestants and Catholics in Parliament which led to the impeachment and subsequent execution of the king's deputy, the earl of Strafford, in Ireland in 1641.

In return for their willingness to support subsidies to the king, Irish Catholics suffered less in the practice of politics and their occupations than in the practice of their religion, but they were neither conciliated nor crushed. In 1641, during the English civil war, a bloody uprising that spread to much of Ireland occurred among the native Irish Catholics of Ulster. In the growing disorder the Catholic Old English combined forces with their coreligionists, the native Irish. A Catholic confederacy was formed at Kilkenny in 1642, but following the victory of the Puritans in England, Oliver Cromwell launched vicious reprisals, including infamous massacres of Catholics at Drogheda and Wexford. Furthermore, in the Act of Settlement of 1652, the Catholic estates of Ireland—with the exception of those in Connaught, the most desolate part of the country—were confiscated and distributed among those who had fought in or financed Cromwell's campaign. Six thousand Catholics lost their estates, and with them their political power. Forty thousand fled into exile, and one hundred thousand were transported to the Americas. Some of their land was returned to Catholics when Charles II was restored to the throne in 1660, but eighty percent of Ireland remained in Protestant hands. The Stuart Plantations and the Cromwellite confiscations had effected an enormous transfer of land, wealth and political power from Catholics to Protestants in every part of Ireland except the southern part of Connaught in the mountainous and inaccessible west.

The Tudor conquest, the Stuart plantations and Cromwell's determination to drive the Irish "to Hell or Connaught" failed to destroy Irish Catholicism. The Catholics would not deny their religion nor could they all be driven out because they were needed as tenants and laborers in areas now owned by Protestants. Many of the new owners were absentee landlords, a class which was to plague Ireland for another two hundred and fifty years, and as O'Farrell notes, "[T]he Irish occupants lived in a land they no longer owned, and the English owners, by and large, owned a land in which they did not live."[4] Some Catholics managed to prosper in trade, an activity not closed to them by law, but they no longer owned the bulk of the land, and Cromwell had destroyed their political role. These facts were only confirmed by the events of 1688 to 1691.

In 1685 the Catholic James II became king, but the Catholics' hopes for emancipation were dashed by his removal from the throne in the English revolution of 1688. James first fled to France, but with the support of Louis XIV in 1689, he went to Ireland to launch a campaign for his restoration. James summoned a parliament in Dublin and took up arms, but he and his Catholic army were defeated by William of Orange at the battle of the Boyne in 1690. In Northern Ireland this is still celebrated as an Irish Protestant victory. At the time the battle had broader implications. James was a surrogate for Louis XIV of France, who was using Ireland as a means to distract William from European concerns. Furthermore, James was more interested in returning to England than in the rights of Irish Catholics. Nevertheless, the war, which ended in 1691, resulted in the expropriation of more Catholic land, so that by the turn of the century, Catholic holdings in Ireland had been reduced to about fifteen percent of the total.

[4] O'Farrell, p. 38.

THE ANGLO–IRISH ASCENDANCY

To protect the power they had won in the seventeenth century, the landowning Protestant elite of Ireland approved a series of Penal Laws in the Irish Parliament. These expelled the Catholic bishops from the country and required priests to register and renounce the pope. The laws denied Catholics the parliamentary franchise, the right to sit in Parliament, to practice law, buy land, maintain schools, send their children abroad to be educated, or own horses worth more than five pounds. The Common Law principle of primogeniture—that the oldest son inherits and keeps intact the estate of his father—was denied to Catholics. Any remaining Catholic estates had to be equally divided among all the sons on the death of an owner, unless there was a Protestant son who would inherit the entire estate. By the late 1770s, Irish Catholics—seventy–five percent of the population—owned only five percent of the land.

The Penal Laws were directed primarily against Catholics, but some, by preferring the Anglican Church of Ireland, worked against Presbyterians, too. There was also a series of British[5] policies which discriminated against Ireland as a whole, both Catholic and Protestant. In the Declaratory Act of 1720, for example, the Parliament at Westminster asserted its right to legislate directly for Ireland—that is, to bypass the Irish Parliament at its discretion. In economics and trade, the mercantilist policies of the government were designed to protect and promote British interests by denying Ireland the right to trade freely with the rest of the world or to develop indigenous industries. One effect of these policies was to encourage large numbers of Catholics to emigrate to the continent, and many Ulster Protestants staged the first large–scale emigration

[5] After the Act of Union with Scotland in 1707 it was better to use the words Britain and British than England or English, although Irish Nationalists always considered England the real enemy.

to America in the late eighteenth century. They were the Scotch–Irish. When simply listed in this way, the Penal Laws and other discriminatory policies are horrifying. Fortunately, they were not strictly enforced. Many of the Catholic clergy evaded registration. Bishops continued to be appointed to Ireland, and children went abroad to study. Ways were found by some to evade the laws concerning landownership—the use of Protestant nominees, for example, or even a nominal conversion—and many Catholics continued to flourish in trade. Neither the Church nor the middle–class commercial interests, nor even Catholic landowners, were completely suppressed. But the laws certainly succeeded in their primary purpose, which was to protect the Protestant ascendency and to deny the Irish Catholics any legitimate role in Irish public life.

The eighteenth century proved to be a century of unflattering contrasts in Ireland, because as the Protestants entered this period of anti–Catholic repression, they simultaneously entered a period of extraordinary accomplishment. This was an age of great Anglo-Irish writers—Swift, Berkeley, Goldsmith, Sheridan and Burke. It was a century of great country houses, and Dublin became a great city—today the finest eighteenth–century city in Britain or Ireland. It was a century of intense political activity by Protestants who had inherited the belief that Ireland was a distinct political community. They spoke of themselves as "the Irish nation," and while this notion excluded the majority of the Catholic population, the Protestant Irish knew that Ireland was distinct from England and they from the English.[6] They could not control the wholly Protestant Irish Parliament because that was dominated by an Irish administration appointed in London and weakened by members who either received patronage from the crown or were the nominees of English absentee landowners. Nevertheless, for a short period at the end of the century, the Anglo–Irish achieved some political success because their agitation for greater political free-

[6] Beckett, pp. 44–83.

dom coincided with a similar movement in the American colonies—the American War of Independence from 1776 to 1781.

Irish Protestants had established volunteer militia groups numbering about forty thousand men, ostensibly to defend the country against France, but when the number of soldiers stationed in Ireland was depleted by the American war, it became clear that the militia was in a position to overwhelm the garrison. The government, therefore, found it prudent to yield to the demands of the Protestant leaders. In 1779, for example, free trade in Irish goods was permitted, and in 1782 Britain—now more concerned with France than with the American colonies—agreed to the demand articulated by Henry Grattan and Henry Flood that there should be an independent Irish Parliament. The British Parliament amended Poyning's Law of 1494 and the Declaratory Act of 1720, so that from 1782 until 1800 only the Irish Parliament was allowed to legislate directly for Ireland, submitting bills for the royal assent without the approval of the British government.

These did not prove to be golden years for Ireland. There were significant improvements for Catholics. For example, most of the Penal Laws were abolished between 1778 and 1792, and Catholics, subject to a property qualification, were allowed to vote from 1793. Furthermore, a Catholic seminary was established at Maynooth, in County Kildare. But in 1795 the Parliament rejected Grattan's relief bill which would have allowed Catholics to sit as members. Furthermore, the Protestant Parliament continued to be influenced by crown patronage, by absentee landlords and by the Irish administration, which was still appointed in London. It was never truly independent and proved incapable of defending Ireland against threats to the peace posed by violent secret societies and by the Society of the United Irishmen, which organized a rebellion with French support in 1798.

THE UNION

William Pitt, the prime minister, concluded that the peace of Ireland and the security of Britain required the abolition of the Irish Parliament. By using crown patronage ("bribery" might be a better word, although such patronage was not an unusual tactic in eighteenth–century politics) and the nominees of absentee landlords, the Irish Parliament was persuaded to vote for the Act of Union in 1800 by a vote of 158 to 115. This act abolished the Irish Parliament and bound Ireland and Britain together in a constitutional union so that from January 1801 the two communities, Ireland and Britain, were merged for the first time in a single parliament. Henceforward, Irish representatives would sit in the House of Commons at Westminster, and representatives of the Irish peerage would sit in the House of Lords.

One reason for the Union was the recognition in Britain that British and Irish interests were not identical. The Protestants of Ireland wanted constitutional and economic independence from Britain and were determined to protect their ascendancy in Ireland against the Catholic majority. The British government, on the other hand, wanted Ireland as a client economy and was willing to grant political concessions to Catholics in order to curb unrest in Ireland that might jeopardize national security and encourage Britain's enemies. A great many Protestants opposed the Union because they feared it would lead to Catholic emancipation, but they soon discovered that as a minority of no more than twenty–five percent in a largely Catholic country, their interests could be better protected from London than from Dublin. They came to see the Union as a fundamental constitutional pact between themselves and the Parliament at Westminster to defend the continued economic, social and political power of the Protestant Irish. When advocating Catholic emancipation, Grattan had asked his fellow countrymen, "Are we to be a Protestant settlement or an

Irish nation?"[7] After the Union, the reply was that they were a Protestant settlement. The Anglo–Irish had genuinely believed themselves to be the Irish nation in the eighteenth century. But in the nineteenth century the term was to be identified almost exclusively with the Catholic Irish, as the Protestants rejected their earlier belief that Ireland was a separate political community and threw their support to the Union.

CONCLUSION

We all have images of the past which are part fact and part imagination. An imperialist is apt to see his empire as a blessing to those he absorbs, whereas his victims see the experience in a different light, idealizing the preimperial past or exaggerating the sufferings under the yoke of the oppressor. Distortions such as these have affected interpretations of the relationship between Ireland and England. We can understand, however, an Irish Nationalist who perceives Anglo–Irish relations as a tale of over seven hundred years of conquest, savage exploitation and repression. The conquest can, indeed, be said to have begun in 1169 or 1170. There were frequent attempts to populate Ireland with "loyalists" from England and to dispossess the indigenous Irish—the Norman and Tudor settlements and the great plantations of the Stuarts. There were bloody campaigns in Ireland by the forces of Elizabeth, Cromwell, and William of Orange. There were calculated attempts to drive out the Gaelic culture and to suppress the Roman Catholic religion—the Statutes of Kilkenny, the Acts of Supremacy and Uniformity, the policy of surrender and regrant, the Cromwellian Act of Settlement, and the Penal Laws. Finally, English mercantilism treated Ireland as an economic colony to be exploited for England's gain.

Without denying these events, we nevertheless ought to qualify them. For example, the Irish were fighting each other before the Normans arrived, and the fighting continued until the completion

[7] O'Farrell, p. 63.

of the conquest in 1603. Irish history, therefore, was not necessarily more bloody because of the intervention of England. Rather than holding Ireland by the sword since 1169, the so–called English conquest was, for more than four hundred years, not a conquest at all. The several attempts to suppress the Gaelic culture and the Catholic religion were unsuccessful because they were not strictly enforced. England preferred a quiet Ireland to a converted one and, in the end, Catholicism survived in Ireland but suffered near–extinction in England, where the authority of the crown could be exercised directly. The Gaelic culture did decline but less because of repressive statutes than because of the political and social dominance of the settlers. The language of law and administration became English, and the sheer weight of the English culture overwhelmed the Irish.

These qualifications may modify our image of English oppression to some degree, but it was oppression nonetheless. Furthermore, it was remarkably fresh in the minds of the men and women who staged the Easter Rising and who perceived English rule in the least favorable light. They believed that nothing less than Irish independence would compensate for the enormity of England's crime. The revolutionaries, however, were not the only Irish nationalists, and the next two chapters will examine how different nationalist groups responded to the facts of English imperialism.

3

Nationalist Movements and Constitutional Nationalism

We should clarify a number of things before we consider nine-teenth–century Catholic Irish Nationalism in the next two chapters. First, Catholics were not united in a single movement. There were in fact three distinct nationalisms. They had overlapping objectives and memberships, it is true, but they were distinct nonetheless. Only two of them, the Revolutionary and Romantic forms, were represented in the 1916 Easter Rising, yet it was the third—Constitutional Nationalism—which dominated the Irish scene in 1914. No one could have predicted with confidence at the time that the other two would be so important or that they would eclipse the constitutional movement in the popular imagination. We cannot put the Easter Rising into its proper perspective unless we recognize this fact. The bulk of this chapter will describe Constitutional Nationalism and its successes. Chapter Four will deal with Revolutionary and Romantic Nationalisms.

Second, Irish Catholicism in 1800 was a very different thing from Irish Catholicism in 1900. The Irish Catholic Church was not a strong institution in 1800, nor were the Irish a particularly devout people. A dramatic change was brought about by Paul Cullan, who was appointed primate of Ireland and archbishop of Armagh in 1849 and archbishop of Dublin in 1852. Under his leadership, the Irish Church became the extraordinarily powerful institution it is today, and the Irish came to be one of the most devout Catholic communities in the world. This devotional revolution need not affect our definition of the Irish Catholic nation because the Irish were defined by their religion—whether they practiced it conscientiously or not—but it did affect the success of Constitutional Nationalism from the 1880s until World War I.

Third, there were many Protestants who shared the national aspirations of the Catholic community, some of whom—Isaac Butt, Charles Stewart Parnell and Douglas Hyde, for example—were outstanding leaders. Nevertheless, they were too few in number for it to be argued that Irish nationalism was ecumenical and represented both communities in Ireland. These Protestants had, as it were, left their own community to join the other side.

In this chapter we will begin to disentangle the complexities of the three forms of nineteenth–century Catholic Irish Nationalism by considering Constitutional Nationalism—the successful movement that ultimately failed. However, we should also clarify what we mean by nationalism.

NATIONALISM AND NATIONALIST MOVEMENTS

In the Europe of the Middle Ages, the mass of the people identified with and were loyal to two bodies, the Roman Catholic Church and their local communities. But as medieval Europe slowly disintegrated, the newly emerging modern states became additional objects of loyalty. This relationship between the people and the state was nationalism, and it reached its highest development in Western Europe in the eighteenth century. However, in the period of the American and French revolutions—at the end of the eighteenth century—nationalism became associated with the democratic theory of the proper relationship between the state and the nation. The state, it was now argued, should be properly constituted. Its authority should flow from the people or the nation.

At first the nation was defined in geographical terms as all the people who lived within the state, but in the nineteenth century it came to be seen in ethnic terms. A nation was defined as a group of people sharing a common identity based on some combination of physical or racial type, language, religion, culture, and shared memories of past glories or tribulations. By this definition several nations might live in a single state or, conversely, several states might share a single nation.

The most important feature of nineteenth–century nationalism was the belief that nations that are not states have the moral right to become states, the right of national self–determination. In Italy and Germany this proved to be an integrating force. In both of them a number of states sharing a single national identity were unified in a single nation state. Elsewhere—in the Austrian and Turkish Empires, for example, and in the United Kingdom following the development of Irish nationalism—it proved to be disintegrative. As Alfred Cobban noted, "Its logical consequence was that any state which could not persuade its people to regard themselves as a single national community, and so become a nation state, must lose its cohesion, and its diverse elements fly apart."[1]

A. D. Smith has argued that nationalism can be both an ideology and a movement.[2] As an ideology, it represents a set of beliefs and values—an identity—which distinguishes one group from another. As a movement, it demands self–determination because only by controlling its own government can a nation be sure of protecting its identity.

A strong nationalist movement does not arrive in a puff of smoke. It has to evolve, and its progress can be evaluated on four dimensions: political, social, cultural and symbolic. First, it must create a political organization with a core of dedicated and talented leaders. These are generally drawn from the educated, urban middle class. Second, it must mobilize support in the population. It must try to break through the conservatism of landowners, the parochialism of the rural peasantry and the inertia of the urban

[1] Alfred Cobban, *The Nation State and National Self–Determination* (London, 1969), p. 42
[2] Anthony D. Smith, ed., *Nationalist Movements* (New York, 1976), chap. 1.

working class. Third, the movement must inculcate the sense that there exists a distinctive national identity and culture. To use a modern phrase, it must engage in consciousness raising. Fourth, a nationalist movement needs to recognize the importance of symbols. In Smith's phrase, it must be "a religion surrogate," something worth dying for.[3] It requires national symbols, myths, heroes and martyrs.

The nineteenth century saw the emergence of many nationalist movements in Europe, and Ireland was very much a part of this development.

CONSTITUTIONAL NATIONALISM

The Constitutional Nationalist movement was in many respects highly successful, but it was never fully mature in the sense of the four–part model of development suggested above. It certainly had a well–developed political organization and a core of dedicated and talented leaders, and it mobilized enormous popular support; but it was relatively unconcerned with cultivating a distinctive Irish national culture, and it did not attach the same importance to symbolism as did Revolutionary or Romantic Nationalism. Revolutionary Nationalists were prepared to die for their image of Ireland, but no one would have sacrificed himself for home rule, the limited form of self–government which became the goal of the Constitutionalists.

Constitutional Nationalism refers to the movement that sought a measure of self–government for Ireland by constitutional means, through parliamentary legislation rather than by revolution. It drew its inspiration from the Parliament which had existed in Dublin for over five hundred years until the Act of Union in 1800. This Parliament had never attained full freedom from England, but it bore witness that Ireland had always been a separate political community. Furthermore, even after the Union, Ireland retained a separate system of administration, unlike Scotland and Wales,

[3] Smith, pp. 8–9.

which were completely absorbed into the United Kingdom. There remained in Ireland after 1800 a representative of the crown, the lord lieutenant, and a chief secretary for Ireland sat in the British cabinet. Half of the government departments operating in Ireland were controlled from Dublin, not London, by a resident under secretary. Irish laws were frequently different from those in Britain and although Ireland had been assigned one hundred members in the House of Commons and thirty–two in the House of Lords, it had many of the characteristics of a colony rather than an integral part of the United Kingdom.

O'CONNELL AND REPEAL

Not unnaturally, the constitutional movement first set its sights on the repeal of the Act of Union and the full recognition of Ireland as a separate political community. It sought the withdrawal of Irish representatives from Westminster and the restoration of a parliament in Dublin with genuine independence and full rights for Catholics. Only the crown would be shared with England.

The first item on the agenda of the constitutional movement was actually not repeal but emancipation. The Penal Laws had largely been abandoned in the last quarter of the eighteenth century, but Catholics were still denied the right to sit in Parliament, to be appointed to the judiciary or to reach the highest ranks in the military or civil service. In 1823, Daniel O'Connell, a County Kerry lawyer, created the Catholic Association and, two years later, developed a fund–raising technique which mobilized millions of supporters for emancipation. Full membership in the association cost one guinea a year, but the poor could become associate members for a shilling, payable in the parishes in monthly installments of one penny.

In 1828 O'Connell demonstrated his power by defeating a member of the government, C. E. Vesey Fitzgerald, for a parliamentary seat in County Clare. As a Catholic, he was unable to take the seat; but with a plentiful supply of funds, the endorsement of the Catholic Church, and the support of millions in Ireland and many in Britain, he was able to mount a great campaign that intimidated the Tory government of the duke of Wellington into conceding Catholic emancipation in 1829. He had mobilized an authentic Irish Catholic nation composed of all classes and supported by the Church.

The government retaliated petulantly by banning the Catholic Association and restricting the franchise to limit the number of Catholic voters in Ireland to about sixteen thousand. But the principle of political rights had been won, and O'Connell had demonstrated that the hitherto passive Irish masses could be mobilized—a harbinger of things to come. The Catholic Association was the forerunner of the modern political party. It was centralized and well funded. Furthermore, it approved parliamentary candidates and withdrew this support—and the certainty of reelection in many districts—if a candidate, once elected, broke his pledge to support the Association.

Once in Parliament, however, O'Connell and his 38 fellow Irish repealers found virtually no British support for their next great project—repeal of the Union—which was defeated by a vote of 529 votes to 38 in the House of Commons in 1834. In 1840, therefore, optimistic that his victory of 1829 could be repeated, O'Connell revived the notion of the great campaign with the Repeal Association which he modeled after the Catholic Association. In 1843 he launched the "Repeal Year." Huge meetings were held, several with more than half a million people. But in October the government banned a major meeting at Clontarf, a Dublin suburb, and arrested O'Connell and six leaders of the new Young Ireland movement for conspiracy. Their subsequent convictions were quashed on appeal, but the government had caused the repeal movement to stall.

The Repeal Association had two million members and O'Connell clearly had the support of the Catholic masses, but his brand of nationalism was beset by problems. The franchise prevented the majority of Catholics from voting, and antirepealers outnumbered repealers in the Irish delegation to the House of Commons. In Ireland a strong minority of bishops was suspicious that O'Connell was too radical, while the Young Irelanders accused him of not being radical enough. In Britain repeal had very little support. Indeed, a Catholic–dominated Irish Parliament was looked upon with horror by a country in which anti–Catholic sentiment, "No Popery," was extremely strong. The majority of British politicians, as well as the press and the middle class, viewed the Irish as lazy, dirty, drunken, violent and priest–ridden. They believed that the source of Ireland's problems was the debased character of its people, not imperialism or absentee landlords. Daniel O'Connell, who received a substantial allowance from the Repeal Association, was represented as a swindler lining his pockets with the penny-a–month "repeal rents."

The repeal movement which was still alive—though far from successful—in 1845, was finally overtaken by events: the onset of the great famine in the fall of 1845; agrarian violence directed by desperate tenant farmers against landowners; Tory policies of coercion designed to curb the violence; and the revolutionary activities of the Young Irelanders. In 1847, in the middle of the crisis, O'Connell died.

Ireland's population had doubled to over eight million in half a century as the introduction of potato culture made possible the division of farms into smaller units, some as small as five acres. These enabled Irish sons and daughters to marry and raise children at a younger age, but their lives were unspeakably miserable. The plight of the Irish peasant may have owed something to the system of absentee Protestant landlords, but the greater part of the blame must be laid to overpopulation and the subsequent pressure on agricultural land. The potato famine destroyed the basis of this subsistence agriculture practiced by Irish peasants. A million or more people died, a million emigrated, and many more were made destitute. The government, motivated by laissez–faire economic doctrines, would do little to alleviate the suffering, and private relief was inadequate. The famine, which lasted until 1851, was an event of unmitigated horror to add to the accumulated miseries already stored in Irish memories. To many people, England—or the English government and English absentee landlords—was responsible, not an abstract economic theory.

HOME RULE

As we will see in Chapter Four, Revolutionary Nationalism was revived in the aftermath of the famine and O'Connell's failure to secure repeal. But there was no major constitutionalist agitation again in Ireland until 1870 when Isaac Butt, a Protestant member of Parliament (M.P.), formed the Home Government Association in Dublin. Neither O'Connell nor Butt were doctrinaire separatists. They believed in Irish self–government because Ireland had been badly governed from London. In addition, as a former Conservative, Butt believed the exploitation of the Catholic masses by absentee landlords was provoking a threat to stability and property in Ireland. Unlike O'Connell, however, Butt did not call for repeal, that is, for co–equal Irish and British parliaments sharing a single crown. Instead, he called for a federal arrangement, or home rule, in which an Irish Parliament and other regional parliaments would be subordinate to the United Kingdom Parliament at Westminster. The home rule movement was to be the most significant political force in Ireland until 1916. In 1873 a Dublin meeting reorganized the Home Government Association into a new Irish mass movement, the Home Rule League, which soon adopted the fund-raising and membership techniques of the Catholic and Repeal Associations. In 1874 fifty–nine home rule Irish Nationalists were elected to Parliament, and the Irish Parliamentary Party was organized, with Butt as chairman, committed solely to Irish home rule.

Earlier attempts to found an independent Irish party, by O'Connell in the 1830s and by Charles Gavan Duffy in the 1850s, had failed. However, Butt's new party ultimately succeeded when Charles Stewart Parnell, a Protestant M.P. from Meath and the son of a liberal landowner, assumed the leadership of the party and the

Home Rule League in 1880 after Butt's death in 1879. The two men had already disagreed strongly over tactics, Butt favoring a single–issue campaign based on home rule and Parnell preferring to tie home rule to land reforms. Furthermore, Butt had opposed the way Parnell and others were deliberately obstructing business in the House of Commons by an astute use of parliamentary rules in order to force the government to deal with the Irish problem. Butt had pursued a policy of moderation and conciliation in an attempt to win Protestant landlords to the home rule movement, but Parnell was prepared to alienate Protestants by supporting Catholic tenant farmers and being more aggressive in Parliament.

Parnell did not have the conservative inhibitions of Butt. He expanded the base of the home rule movement and secured new sources of funds. For example, in 1880 he went to the United States, his mother's birthplace, where he cooperated with Revolutionary Nationalists in the Irish–American organization, the Clan na Gael, to raise £20,000. From that time on, the Irish in America became the most important source of financial support for Constitutional Nationalism. The election expenses of the Irish Party and subsistence allowances for many of its members could now be paid. However, linking home rule to land reform—the dominant political issue for Irish Catholics and a long standing concern of the Catholic Church—was the key to Parnell's success.

The great majority of Catholic farmers were tenants of Protestant landowners and had long suffered from an exploitative land tenure system which, by custom, was not practiced in Ulster. If they improved their farms through hard work and investment, their landlords could charge higher rents. Furthermore, they could be evicted without compensation for their improvements. Since the eighteenth century, the Irish countryside had been the scene of organized violence by secret societies directed against landlords and agents who abused the system. The population explosion had exacerbated the problem as holdings were subdivided time and again down to five–acre plots, but the famine drastically cut the Irish population and the pressure on the land. The number of peasant and marginal farmers declined and farmers became more prosperous; but bad harvests between 1877 and 1879 revived the agrarian unrest of the past. Emmet Larkin defines the Catholic tenant farmers holding more than thirty acres as the "nation-forming class."[4] They were first mobilized politically by Daniel O'Connell in the 1820s, and Parnell was able to tie their unrest to Constitutional Nationalism once again. In 1879 he helped Michael Davitt, a former revolutionary who had returned to Ireland from exile in America, to found the National Land League. Parnell became president, and in 1880, the Irish Parliamentary Party joined the land agitation. After the Land League was banned by the government, its successor—the Irish National League, founded in 1882—became the popular arm of Constitutional Nationalism in virtually every Catholic parish in Ireland, replacing the Home Rule League.

The Land League operated in the middle ground between Constitutional Nationalism and revolutionary violence. It demanded legislation to guarantee fair rents, security of tenure and the right of a tenant to sell his tenancy for the value of the improvements he had made. But it also organized boycotts (named after Captain Boycott, a land agent in County Mayo), which were directed against exploiting landlords and farmers who took over the farms of evicted tenants. It followed the policy outlined by James Fintan Lalor, who argued in the 1840s that civil disobedience and the nonpayment of rents would destroy landlordism. Landlords, the League, and the police were soon involved in violent disputes throughout the country.

In March 1880, a general election returned sixty–one home rule M.P.'s to Parliament. It also returned the Liberals and William Gladstone to power. Gladstone's earlier government (1868–1874) had tried to discourage Irish nationalism by legislating several Irish reforms, notably the disestablishment of the Anglican Church of Ireland in 1869 and an ineffective Irish Land Act in 1870. The

[4] Emmet Larkin, "Church, State, and Nation in Modern Ireland," *American Historical Review* 80: 5 (December 1975): 1244–1276.

government was actually brought down on an Irish issue in 1874 when a bill to transform Dublin University into a national university with separate sectarian colleges was defeated in the House of Commons, in large part because the Irish bishops wanted a completely independent Catholic university. However, Gladstone's return to office meant that Parnell would be dealing with a man who had shown some sympathy for Ireland's problems.

Their relationship was not immediately satisfactory. Gladstone's 1881 Land Act enacted most of the demands of the Land League, but Parnell rejected it because it neglected the serious problem of arrears of rent owed by thousands of farmers. The League was banned that year for its campaign of intimidation, and Parnell himself was imprisoned in Kilmainham Prison, Dublin, for his role in the movement. After the so-called Kilmainhaim Treaty of 1882, Parnell was released. He had agreed to support the Land Act, but Gladstone had agreed to amend it to pay arrears of rent so that these farmers could benefit from its terms. Parnell also agreed that the Irish party would support the Liberal government. This did not completely end the land agitation, because rents were systematically withheld between 1886 and 1889 in the Plan of Campaign; but it cemented the relationship between land reform and Constitutional Nationalism and laid the groundwork for the long-term alliance with the Liberals.

On his release, Parnell—now a hero in Ireland—reorganized the home rule movement and managed to come to terms with the Catholic Church. The majority of the bishops had opposed the radical Land League, and Cardinal Cullan of Dublin had long used his power to forestall an independent Irish party, preferring to work with the Liberals. But, in effect, a deal was struck between 1884 and 1886. The Church would endorse the Irish Party, home rule, and a plan of land purchase for tenant farmers, while the party would support the demand that the education of Catholics, at every level, should be controlled by the Church.

In 1885 the Irish Party helped to force Gladstone out of office by voting with the Conservatives in the House of Commons, and at the subsequent general election, eighty-six home rule M.P.'s were elected. The full effect of the successive extensions of the franchise was felt as Catholic voters took permanent control of three-quarters of Ireland. The home rule members now held the balance in the House of Commons because neither the Liberals nor the Conservatives had an overall majority, and no government could be formed without Irish support. This was all the more important because the Irish, who had been deliberately under-represented in 1800, were now, since the famine and massive emigrations, overrepresented. Furthermore, Parnell had under his command the first modern, disciplined party in parliamentary history—an awesome weapon. In December 1885, Parnell threw his support to Gladstone who announced his support for home rule. His first Home Rule Bill was introduced in April 1886.

The Home Rule Bill will be considered in some detail in Chapter Six, but for the moment we must recognize Parnell's achievement. Though a Protestant himself, he had succeeded in organizing the members of Parliament from Catholic Ireland into a highly disciplined and aggressive party. By linking home rule and land reform, he had ensured the support of the Catholic tenant farmers—the most important social class in Ireland—and had built a grass roots political network with millions of supporters. He had also secured the cooperation of the Catholic bishops. Finally, Parnell had firmly established the relationship between the Catholic Irish nation and a future Irish state. "By 1886," writes Emmet Larkin, "the British state had lost the great game it had played for so many centuries in Ireland. An Irish state had not only been created in the minds of most Irishmen, but the national and local political apparatus necessary to the functioning of that state was operative."[5] The 1886 Home Rule Bill, which demonstrated that the hitherto sacrosanct Union was now negotiable, meant that the ratification of the Irish state by the British Parliament appeared to be only a matter of time.

It is true that Parnell had achieved this success by political

[5] Larkin, p. 1266.

organization in Ireland and party discipline in the House of Commons, but always lurking in the background was the threat of violence. The Land League had already intimidated the government into concessions and might be mobilized again. In addition, Revolutionary Nationalists in Ireland and America discovered that Parnell was so dominant a leader that they had no choice but to support him. The "New Departure" policy of 1879, for example, had involved an alliance between Parnell, Michael Davitt of the Land League and John Devoy of the revolutionary Clan na Gael, and although Parnell was not a revolutionary himself, he had the support of men much more violent than he. This fact formed a constant and rather menacing backdrop to his negotiations with the Liberals.

The home rule movement that Parnell built survived until World War I, consistently winning the support of the mass of Irish voters and sending more than eighty home rule members to Parliament. It achieved this despite a great leadership crisis in 1890 after the husband of Parnell's mistress, Katherine O'Shea, cited Parnell in his divorce suit. It was a measure of Parnell's enormous stature in the movement that he was not immediately denounced by his followers, most of whom were Catholics; and it was a measure of his poor judgment in the case that he clung to the leadership and refused to resign. His defeat was finally forced when Gladstone, whose support was essential for home rule, repudiated him. The Irish Party then divided on the issue. Two–thirds of the party rejected Parnell and installed Justin McCarthy as the parliamentary leader. The minority, loyal to Parnell and resentful of Gladstone's interference, followed John Redmond. Parnell himself contracted rheumatic fever during a campaign to reassert his position in Ireland and died in October 1891.

Parnell's death did not heal the rift in the party, and it was not until 1900 that the factions came together again. A new popular organization founded in 1898, the United Irish League, was the medium for their reunion, which saw the majority anti–Parnellite leader, John Dillon, generously yielding to the Parnellite, John

Redmond. The reunion was extremely successful, and it is not true, as Dangerfield asserts, that Parnell took home rule with him to the grave, from which it emerged only briefly in 1912.[6] The parliamentary agitation was not dead. The Irish had always depended on a favorable distribution of power in the House of Commons for their parliamentary victories, and when this distribution occurred again in 1910, they were prepared. In the intervening years, as a parliamentary party, as a mass movement in Ireland and America, and with renewed financial support from the United States, Constitutional Nationalism marched confidently towards what it regarded as the certain victory of home rule, virtually unchallenged by the revolutionaries who took the field in 1916.

Hand in hand with its progress in the field of party politics, Constitutional Nationalism was making giant strides in the Irish administration, particularly after the return of a Liberal government in 1906. When Parnell became leader of the movement in 1880, there was only one Catholic among forty–one heads of departments in Ireland. By 1914 more than half of the by then forty–eight departments were headed by Catholics or Protestant supporters of home rule, and there was an equal division of Catholics and Protestants on the Supreme Court bench. Ireland was no longer a Unionist dictatorship. The administration for an Irish state, built upon the long–standing existence of a separate political community in Ireland, was already established.

CONCLUSION

There were marked differences between the constitutional agitations of Parnell and Redmond. Parnell himself was dead, of course, and Redmond was an uninspiring, though competent, leader. But more important was the fact that Constitutional Nationalism was now divorced from incipient violence. The Conservatives' Land Act of 1903 had ended the association with agrarian radicalism, and the revolutionary movement was, as we shall see,

[6] George Dangerfield, *The Damnable Question* (Boston, 1976), p. 23.

virtually silent if not totally dormant. The very success of constitutionalism had blunted its cutting edge, which had always been its tacit relationlship with the men of violence. Parnell knew how to manipulate this threat of violence, but by temperament and circumstance, Redmond was incapable of doing so. As Oliver Mac-Donagh suggests, "Redmond was inhibited by his own beliefs from enlisting Irish militancy as an ally."[7] We shall see in Chapter Six that he paid a heavy price for his sensitivity when the victory of home rule was snatched from him by militant Protestants in 1914.

[7] Oliver MacDonagh, *Ireland* (Englewood Cliffs, N.J., 1968), p. 57.

4

Revolutionary and Romantic Nationalism

The momentum of Constitutional Nationalism was checked in 1914, for reasons which we will explore in Chapter Six. "Checked" is certainly a more appropriate word than "destroyed" because constitutionalism deeply influenced the parliamentary and bureaucratic institutions as well as the political behavior of the independent Ireland that emerged from the War of Independence in 1922. But it was overshadowed, of course, by the revolutionary movement. In this chapter we will turn to Revolutionary Nationalism and its close relation, Romantic Nationalism.

REVOLUTIONARY NATIONALISM

The Easter Rising was the most important step in Irish revolutionary history, but the revolutionary movement always represented a small minority of the population. Like its constitutional counterpart, it was never fully mature in the sense of the four–part model of development described at the beginning of Chapter Three. It attracted dedicated leaders, but they were, for the most part, poor organizers and were frequently divided among themselves. As Malcolm Brown says, "Even the warmest friend of Ireland must confess that its revolutionary staff work throughout history was never better than slovenly."[1] Furthermore, it was never a popular movement. Its active supporters were always few. Also, some Revolutionary Nationalists—particularly the Young Irelanders—were concerned with Irish history and culture, but this was not a consistent theme in the movement. Many were primarily motivated by their hostility toward England rather than any really substantial vision of a new Ireland. John Mitchel, one of their number, wrote, "I have found that there was perhaps less of love in [the movement] than hate. . . ."[2] And finally, they were extremely adept at manipulating symbols—those heroes and martyrs of Irish history. On special occasions, they found that they could mobilize support from large numbers of people whose nationalism was latent or relatively passive, people who generally expressed themselves through the constitutional movement.

Revolutionary Nationalism was committed to the establishment, by force, of an independent Irish republic. England would have to be driven out of Ireland because it would never leave willingly. It began with the Society of United Irishmen, founded in 1791 by middle–class, urban Protestants who included Wolfe Tone and Robert Emmet. Henry Grattan, who led the agitation for an independent Irish Parliament in 1782, was inspired by the American Revolution, but the United Irishmen were inspired by the French Revolution. Their aims were not at first revolutionary and included Catholic emancipation, universal suffrage and parliamentary reform, but the character of the movement soon changed. The society became involved with violent, agrarian secret societies—the Catholic "Defenders" and the Protestant "Peep O'Day Boys"—and began to intrigue with France which was at war with England. It was forced underground in 1794 after government informers learned of secret negotiations with the French government.

Wolfe Tone was one of a number of leaders who fled Ireland in

[1] Malcolm Brown, *The Politics of Irish Literature* (Seattle, 1972), p. 21.
[2] Thomas Flanagan, "Rebellion and Style: John Mitchel and the Jail Journal," *Irish University Review* 1 (Autumn 1970): 4–5.

1794. He emigrated, permanently he thought, to the United States, but he was given the task of opening negotiations with France through its representatives in America. In January 1796, he went to France to encourage and plan a French invasion of Ireland. The French were led to believe that Ireland was seething with revolution, but in fact the United Irishmen were poorly organized and the uncoordinated agrarian agitation was primarily concerned with the redress of rural grievances, not with revolution and independence. Furthermore, agrarian violence often became sectarian violence as the Protestant Peep O'Day Boys, who were reorganized as the Orange Society in 1795, attacked Catholic targets, for which the Catholic Defenders replied in kind. Revolution was further inhibited by the government, which legislated the Insurrection Act of 1796 and suspended habeas corpus in its zeal to suppress the Defenders. Nevertheless, in December 1796, Wolfe Tone and a fleet of ships carrying fourteen thousand Frenchmen sailed for Bantry Bay in Ireland. Heavy storms prevented any troop landings, which was fortunate for France since Ireland was not organized for a rebellion and a spontaneous uprising was out of the question.

A rebellion did occur in May 1798, but it, too, was a failure, developing as a series of uncoordinated actions which were easily and brutally suppressed by early July. Only in Wexford—where it attracted approximately thirty thousand volunteers—was there a significant response, and even there the rising was aimless and poorly led. When French troops landed at Killala in August, they found virtually no revolutionary activity and were captured within weeks. Wolfe Tone himself sailed from France in September and was captured at sea. He joined about seventy other leaders of the United Irishmen in prison and became a martyr to the cause of Irish freedom when he died, after a suicide attempt in November 1798.

In 1803 there was another abortive United Irish rising in Dublin. Three thousand volunteers were expected to attack Dublin Castle during the evening of July 23, but only about three hundred turned out, and Robert Emmet led a confused attack which was over within a few hours. As Robert Kee writes, "The plan itself was reasonable and practical, its execution lamentable to the point of farce."[3] But Emmet was martyred by execution. His contribution to the cause lay in his heroic example and inspiring speech from the dock which concluded, "When my country takes her place among the nations of the earth, then, and not till then, let my epitaph be written."[4] He joined Wolfe Tone in the revolutionary pantheon.

The United Irishmen were members of the Protestant ascendancy who were few in number and mobilized little popular support. They were Irish Jacobins, motivated by the democratic and egalitarian ideas of the French revolution, not by the history, culture or national identity of their native land. They failed but became heroes and martyrs and an inspiration for the very different class of Irish nationalists which was to follow in 1916.

Revolutionary Nationalism was not revived until 1848, the year of revolution in Europe. Its instrument was the Young Ireland movement, which was more distinguished by its contribution to Romantic Nationalism—as we shall see—than for its revolutionary skill. Young Ireland was associated with O'Connell's repeal agitation in the early 1840s. But it differed in its commitment to an Irish cultural revival, in its insistence that Ireland should be completely free of the English connection, and in its belief that violence might be necessary to achieve Irish freedom. It was only after O'Connell's death during the famine in 1847 that the revolutionary strain became dominant. John Mitchel, formerly the editor of the Young Ireland newspaper, the *Nation*, led the way. His new paper, the *United Irishman*, founded in January 1848, urged that preparations should be made for a revolution. Mitchel was soon arrested and was convicted in May. He was transported to a penal colony in Australia from which he was rescued by an Irish–American expedition in 1853.

[3] Robert Kee, *The Green Flag* (New York, 1972), p. 164.
[4] Kee, p. 168.

More arrests followed. The *Nation* was suppressed, habeas corpus was suspended, and martial law was imposed in several parts of Ireland. In May a small rebellion occurred, provoked by government coercion and repression. It was yet another failure—an unplanned revolution disowned by the Catholic Church, unsupported by the Irish people and degenerating into farce. The small force led by William Smith O'Brien in County Tipperary was quickly defeated in what was disparagingly but justifiably called "the battle of the Widow McCormack's cabbage plot."[5]

The Young Irelanders were men of considerable talent who would have formed a distinguished political elite in any country, but they were dispersed around the world. O'Brien, John Martin, T. B. McManus, and Thomas Meagher were transported, like Mitchel, to Australia. McManus and Meagher joined Mitchel by escaping to America where Meagher served as a brigadier general in the Union army, the commander of an Irish–American brigade, before becoming governor of the Montana territory. Darcy McGee fled to Canada where he became a minister in the dominion government before being murdered by an Irish extremist in 1868. James Stephens and John O'Mahony fled to France, and O'Mahony went on to America. Charles Gaven Duffy managed to escape conviction, despite being prosecuted several times. He was at heart a home ruler not a revolutionary, and he served in the House of Commons in the 1850s, but even he emigrated to Australia. He became prime minister of the colony of Victoria before returning to Ireland as an old man.

Many Young Irelanders were sentenced to death, but the sentences were commuted. The government would not make martyrs, even if O'Brien did declare that he would refuse clemency. They failed as revolutionaries and certainly failed to mobilize popular opinion, but they made an extraordinary contribution to the definition of an Irish national culture. Although they were not executed,

---

[5] Kee, pp. 284–286; Lawrence McCaffrey, *Ireland: From Colony to Nation State* (Englewood Cliffs, N.J., 1979), p. 69.

the Rising made them heroes and their assorted exiles made them martyrs of a sort.

For many Young Irelanders, 1848 was a solitary revolutionary fling, but for some it marked a new direction. In 1858, for example, James Stephens founded the Irish Republican Brotherhood (I.R.B.) to work for an independent Irish Republic by physical force. In the United States a related organization, the Fenian Brotherhood, was founded by John O'Mahony. Both organizations came to be known as the Fenians. Fenianism was distinctive in that it was both Irish and Irish American, and from 1873 the two branches were united by a single revolutionary directory with seven members. The movement actually had more members in America, where it could operate openly among the enormous number of postfamine immigrants, than it did in Ireland, where it had to operate in secret. In both countries it was primarily a proletarian movement with most members drawn from people of little or no property—laborers, marginal farmers, mechanics, clerks and so on. It also had considerable support among enlisted Irishmen in the British army. The members appear to have been motivated primarily by a visceral hatred of England, but this is not to say that there were not those with more sophisticated tastes. John O'Leary, for example, who had been a Young Irelander and led the I.R.B. for many years before his death in 1907, was an ardent collector of Irish literature and history and had a profound influence on the young W. B. Yeats. As Malcolm Brown argues, "He believed that Irish poetry must be national, and Irish nationalism poetic."[6] However, the movement as a whole was single–minded in its commitment to the establishment of an Irish Republic.

Fenianism was opposed by Constitutional Nationalists, by many of the survivors of Young Ireland, and most importantly by the Catholic Church, which condemned its secrecy and feared its radical and revolutionary influence among the poor. The Fenians were, with few exceptions, devout Catholics themselves but either kept their membership a secret from their priests, withdrew from

[6] Brown, p. 8.

the Church or found sympathetic priests in whom to confide. The Roman Catholic Church has always opposed secret societies and revolutionary violence in Ireland, but one of the characteristics of Revolutionary Nationalists, even today, has been their refusal to allow the Church to influence this part of their lives. The ultimate evidence of their commitment to their country has been their rejection of the Church on this one issue, even in the face of excommunication.

Many of the more than one hundred thousand Irish Americans who fought in the American Civil War became Fenians, and some returned to Ireland after the war to participate in a rising. But the government had informers in the movement on both sides of the Atlantic and intervened several times to forestall action. In September 1865, for example, Jeremiah O'Donovan Rossa, John O'Leary, Charles Kickham, Thomas Luby and others were arrested. In November James Stephens was captured. He escaped within weeks and fled to America, but in February 1866, seven hundred more suspected Fenians were arrested and imprisoned without trial. John Devoy, who was later to lead the revolutionary movement in America for many years and helped to plan the Easter Rising, was imprisoned in Ireland as a Fenian from 1866 to 1871.

The long anticipated Fenian rising in Ireland did not occur until February and March 1867 when several thousand men, led by an Irish–American, Thomas J. Kelly, attempted risings in Dublin, Cork, Tipperary, and elsewhere. The government suppressed them in a few days, with little loss of life. An American supply ship, the *Erin's Hope*, did not arrive until May. One hundred and sixty Fenians were finally convicted for their parts in the Rising, but there were no executions. The government did not want to create Fenian martyrs.

In America, where anti–British sentiment was high after the Civil War, the Fenian Brotherhood had a career which was possibly more spectacular. It operated more or less openly, with parades and drills. An invasion of Ireland was impossible, but on May 31, 1886, fifteen hundred Fenians invaded Canada at Niagara. The invasion was quickly repelled, and two other raids across the border, in 1870 and 1871, were equally aborted.

The Fenian Brotherhood died in the early 1870s. The Church in America had joined the Irish Church in banning the organization, the American government became less tolerant of Fenian activities as relations with Britain improved, and the Fenian leadership was constantly torn by dissension. The organization was succeeded by the Clan na Gael, which had been founded in 1867.

The revolutionary movement survived in both Ireland and America because there were always men who believed in violence as the only way. For example, Lord Frederick Cavendish, the chief secretary, and T. H. Burke, his under secretary, were assassinated in Phoenix Park in 1882. But there was no significant revolutionary activity in Ireland for forty years after the 1867 Rising. The Clan na Gael was somewhat more active in America, although riddled by internal conflicts. Some members supported Parnell and the Irish Land League, but others, led by O'Donovan Rossa, organized a campaign of dynamite sabotage in England in the 1880s that was the forerunner of the I.R.A. terrorism of modern times.

Revolutionary Nationalism in the Fenian tradition was revived in America by a reorganization of the Clan na Gael in 1900, and in 1907 the Clan sent Tom Clarke back to Ireland. He was a convicted dynamiter who had been released in 1898 after serving fifteen years in an English prison. His task was to put new life into the secret I.R.B. which had been slumbering for many years. He joined a new, young leadership group which included Denis McCullough, Bulmer Hobson, Sean MacDiarmada, P. S. O'Hegarty and others, but the organization probably numbered fewer than two thousand members and was maintained in part by grants from the Clan na Gael. It was incapable of a rising, but its most successful policy was to infiltrate its members into leading positions in other nationalist organizations, one of which was Sinn Fein.

Sinn Fein owed its existence to Arthur Griffith, the editor of the *United Irishman*, first published in 1899. Griffith's contribution was to use his newspaper to popularize and expand a strategy first suggested by the Young Irelanders and O'Connell, that is the systematic withdrawal of Irish representatives from Westminster; and the creation, *de facto*, of a parallel system of Irish government and law which would deny England the power to actually govern Ireland. He argued that Ireland should follow the example of the Hungarian nationalists who had won independence in 1861, within the framework of the dual Austro–Hungarian monarchy, by refusing to send Hungarian members to the Austrian Imperial Parliament. In 1900 he formed an organization, Cumann na nGaedheal, to promote his views; and in 1905 joined with another loose nationalist group organized by members of the I.R.B., the Dungannon Clubs, to form Sinn Fein, a name drawn from the Irish word for "ourselves."

Sinn Fein was no match for the constitutional movement and its candidate for parliament was soundly beaten in a 1908 by-election, but it did attract considerable support, reaching a peak in the period between 1908 and 1910. More important, however, it became, with Griffith's approval, a front for revolutionary separatism. Indeed, the Easter Rising was immediately christened "the Sinn Fein Rebellion" in the press and by the government although the organization had played no formal role at all. After the Rising it was reorganized officially as the political wing of the revolutionary movement, and it set about the strategy of withdrawal from Westminster which Griffith had outlined earlier. It remains today the political wing of the Irish Republican Army.

The I.R.B. continued its own separate and secret existence. In 1910, for example, it launched a newspaper, *Irish Freedom*, to carry its message to the public, but it would have accomplished nothing if the situation in Ireland had not changed dramatically between 1912 and 1914. As we shall see in Chapter Six, Constitutional Nationalism was poised for the victory of home rule in Parliament in 1913 when the Ulster Protestants organized a paramilitary force, the Ulster Volunteers, to resist home rule by force. Members of the I.R.B. were critically important the following November in organizing the Nationalists' reply, the Irish Volunteers. This organization was first suggested by an essentially moderate man, Eoin MacNeill, professor of early Irish history at University College Dublin, but a third of its organizing committee was made up of members of the secret I.R.B. The Irish Volunteers quickly grew, and in 1914 John Redmond, who saw it as a threat to the authority of the Irish Party, forced his nominees into a commanding position on the committee of the organization. But what he and the chairman of the Volunteers, MacNeill, did not know was that key positions in the command structure were held by members of the I.R.B., men such as Patrick Pearse, SeanMacDiarmada, The O'Rahilly,[7] and Bulmer Hobson. It was they who led a small number of the Volunteers into the Easter Rising in 1916.

ROMANTIC NATIONALISM

Patrick Pearse, a member of the I.R.B., was one of many who had first been inspired not by the revolutionary tradition of the Fenians but by another tradition, Romantic Nationalism. Whereas the constitutional movement was primarily concerned with establishing a government which would be more responsive to Irish needs, and the revolutionary movement was motivated by a hatred for England and a disdain for constitutional agitation, the romantic movement approached nationalism from the perspective of the national culture. Its purpose was to revive, or even to create, a distinctive and indigenous Irish culture. In terms of the four–part model of development described earlier, Romantic Nationalism eschewed political organization as such although it had a profound impact on Irish politics. It did seek to mobilize popular support but in order to promote the sense of a distinctive Irish culture and identify and cultivate nationalist symbols and the nationalist spirit.

Roman Catholicism had given the majority of the Irish people

---

[7] "The" is an old Irish title representing the senior living descendant of a Clan chieftain.

their sense of corporate identity in the nineteenth century, but from the time of the emancipation movement in the 1820s, the Church had been associated with constitutionalism and parliamentary reform. Romantic Nationalism sought a definition of the Irish nation which went far beyond religion and the constitution.

In 1842, three founders of Young Ireland—a Protestant, Thomas Davis, and two Catholics, John B. Dillon and Charles Gavan Duffy—began to publish the weekly newspaper, *Nation*, to expound their view that Ireland was both a geographical and a spiritual entity. They attacked the materialism of industrial and commercial England and the introduction of its values into Ireland. The Irish, they argued, possessed a history, a heritage and a culture of their own. The *Nation* published Irish prose and poetry and essays on history, ethnography and antiquities. It extolled the heroic image of ancient Ireland and urged the preservation of the Irish language, then spoken by fewer than a quarter of the population. England was accused of having deprived the Irish not only of their culture but of the cultural foundations of the Irish nation itself. Without a culture, there could be no nation. Their purpose, therefore, was to build—or rebuild—an Irish nation by recreating an Irish culture.

Central to the Young Ireland argument was the view that Irish nationality transcended religion and race. Protestants and Catholics were held to be one in the Irish nation. Davis spoke of Ireland as "a nation once again," and of wanting "to inflame and purify" the Irish with a "lofty and heroic love of country."[8] But his emphasis upon a Gaelic Ireland was bound to divide the two Irish communities, the Gaelic and the Anglo–Irish.

The Young Irelanders split from O'Connell's repeal movement by endorsing nonsectarian education. O'Connell, who was anxious not to alienate the Church, had decided to support a Church–controlled education system for Catholics, but the Young Irelanders saw sectarianism as divisive and destructive of the unity of the Irish nation. Furthermore, although O'Connell spoke Irish, he ar-

[8] Kee, pp. 196–198.

gued that its preservation hampered the intellectual and economic development of Ireland. His nationalism was utilitarian not cultural.

In 1847 the Young Irelanders founded the Irish Confederation as a popular organization to challenge O'Connell's Repeal Association—with little success—and in 1848 they turned to revolution, albeit reluctantly. The *Nation* had consistently praised the warrior heroes of ancient Ireland and the men of 1798 and 1803, but it appears that the young Irelanders were not, by instinct or aptitude, revolutionaries themselves. Their rising was decisively crushed, but their example inspired the revolutionaries of 1916 and the *Nation's* message that Ireland was a cultural and spiritual entity proved to be extraordinarily influential. As McCaffrey argues, "Davis, Dillon and Duffy gave Irish nationalism the most powerful and influential newspaper voice it ever had or ever would have, and they contributed traditions and values that would permanently shape its character."[9]

Romantic Nationalism revived in a number of forms in the 1880s and 1890s, ironically, just as Ireland's material grievances were being resolved by reforms in land tenure, local government and education. One example was the Gaelic Athletic Association, founded in the west of Ireland by Michael Cusack in 1884. It promoted Irish games such as Gaelic football and hurling and forbade its members to play English games such as soccer or cricket. It became extremely influential in rural Ireland.

The Gaelic League, founded in 1893, appealed to a different group of people: middle class, well educated and urban. It promoted the study and practice of the Irish language, literature and music, each of which had steadily declined in the years since the conquest. Indeed, Irish was now the native language only of peasants in the remote west and southwest of the island. Many of the leaders of 1916, including Pearse and Eamon de Valera, were introduced to Irish Nationalism through their membership in the

[9] Lawrence McCaffrey, *The Irish Question, 1800–1922* (Lexington, 1968), p. 41.

Gaelic League, which had accumulated more than six hundred branches and many thousands of dedicated supporters by 1908. By 1910 every student at the National University of Ireland was required to matriculate in Irish.

A rather different cultural development was the Irish literary revival. In the 1890s a group of writers, predominantly Protestant and from the upper class, founded a literary movement in the belief that Ireland had suffered from English cultural imperialism and was in need of an indigenous culture. They differed from the Gaelic movement in believing that the literary medium could be English. The revival was associated with the National Literary Society, founded in Dublin in 1892, and the Abbey Theater, founded by W. B. Yeats and Lady Gregory in 1904. It attracted other writers such as J. M. Synge, G. W. Russell (AE) and George Moore. For inspiration and themes, they turned to Irish peasant life—to those whose culture was least affected by exposure to England—and to the history, sagas, fairy tales and oral folklore of Ireland. They drew heavily from the research of Standish O'Grady who, in Dangerfield's phrase, had begun "unlocking one of the richest mythologies in Europe" in the 1880s.[10]

The movement attracted writers of international stature and cosmopolitan standards who wanted to create an indigenous literature in English from Irish sources, but their work was often controversial. They encountered the hostility of the Catholic hierarchy, of Arthur Griffith and Sinn Fein, and of many members of the Gaelic League who represented a narrow, parochial and idealized view of Irish life. They were accused of misrepresenting Irish womanhood, of demeaning Irish peasants, of undermining Catholic morals and of neglecting the Irish language, the very heart of a national culture. Eager patriots, anxious to protect the reputation of the Irish nation as they saw it, staged protests—the "Playboy Riots"—when the Abbey Theatre staged Synge's play, *The Playboy of the Western World*, in 1907.

The issue, in a fundamental sense, was one of artistic freedom.

[10] George Dangerfield, *The Damnable Question* (Boston, 1976), p. 31.

The Church believed that art should be an instrument of religious and moral education. Many nationalists believed it should be an instrument of national propaganda. Yeats had battled since the 1890s for the freedom of the artist in Ireland, and he refused to build an Irish literature or an Irish nation on foundations of ignorance or deceit. However, by 1910 he and his colleagues had lost what F. S. L. Lyons calls, "the battle of the two civilizations."[11] The narrow parochialists came to dominate Irish literature until recent times, and some of Ireland's most respected writers—James Joyce, Sean O'Casey and Samuel Becket, for example—found that they could only work abroad, though their art was always inspired by their Irishness.

The literary revival was not sustained, but it did contribute to a growing sense of national identity and in later years was accepted as one of the cultural glories of Ireland. Together with the Gaelic League and the Gaelic Athletic Association, it encouraged the notion that Ireland possessed a distinctive culture with traditions and customs quite separate from England.

In one critical respect, however, the Gaelic revival differed from the literary revival. Its nationalism was explicitly Gaelic and was tied to the ancient culture of the Catholic majority. Douglas Hyde, one of the founders of the Gaelic League and a Protestant himself, claimed to be nonsectarian; but his determination to make Irish the national language and, in his phrase, to "de-Anglicize" Ireland had revolutionary implications for the quarter of the nation that denied it was Irish in the Gaelic sense. His was the message of Thomas Davis and Young Ireland. It was now known as "Irish Ireland," and it was nativistic: its definition of the nation was exclusive, not inclusive. Rather than seeking a framework which might accommodate all Irishmen, it simply excluded—as the Protestant nation had done in the eighteenth century—those who would not conform to its definition of the Irish. This exclusive definition alienated the members of the literary revival, most of whom were Anglo-Irish and were therefore divorced by birth

[11] F. S. L. Lyons, *Ireland Since the Famine* (London, 1971), pp. 219–242.

from its central assumptions. The irony is that Irish Ireland has never been accepted by the majority of the Catholic population itself, even when from the 1920s the weight of the Irish state and its educational system was thrown into battle. A Gaelic Ireland has certainly inspired many Irish men and women, in several generations, but its success has been as a symbol of Ireland's separation from England and not as a particularly vital force in Irish life.

Patrick Pearse was, in the context of the Easter Rising, the most distinguished product of the Gaelic revival. In 1908 he founded a bilingual school in Dublin, St. Edna's, which stressed Irish language, history, culture and games. Pearse believed that the educational system imposed on Ireland by England had crushed the Irish national spirit. Liberation could only be achieved by the overthrow of English education and ultimately by the overthrow of English imperialism. Pearse was obsessed by the heroic deed and the heroic image. Fenians might hope to overthrow England by an armed rising, but Pearse had a mystical and sacrificial vision. Ireland could only be reborn through the blood sacrifice of a few. Bloodshed, he argued, "is a cleansing thing and the nation which regards it as the final horror has lost its manhood."[12]

Pearse joined the I.R.B. in 1913 and was one of those who organized the Irish Volunteers that year. Indeed, three of the Volunteer directors—Pearse, director of military organization, Thomas MacDonagh, director of military training, and Joseph Plunkett, director of military operations—shared the same mystical nationalism. All were Gaelic enthusiasts, all were poets and all believed in the blood sacrifice. At the Dublin funeral of the old Fenian, O'Donovan Rossa—an extraordinary symbolic act manipulated by the I.R.B.—Pearse declared, "Life springs from death; and from the graves of patriot men and women spring living nations."[13] He did not expect to defeat the English in battle. Indeed, victory would come, as it came for Christ, from not surviv-

[12] Lyons, p. 336.
[13] Patrick Pearse, *The Best of Pearse*, edited by Proinsias Mac Aonghusa and Liam Ó Réagáin (Cork, 1967), p. 134.

ing, from the sacrifice and the example. As McDara says in Pearse's play, *The Singer*, "One man can free a people as one Man redeemed the world."[14] In Pearse, then, was combined the heroic sacrifice of Wolfe Tone and Robert Emmet, the cultural and spiritual vision of Thomas Davis and the Gaelic League, the messianic image of Christ, and the revolutionary zeal of the Fenians. It proved to be an extraordinarily volatile mixture. Malcolm Brown wrote that by the 1840s Irish Nationalists had learned that their opportunities must be made as well as waited for. "Flaming words, redemptive symbology—these were essential, granted; and Irish modes in religion, language, and cultural tradition had to be collected, arrayed and made battle-ready. But the brother-nationalists of Wales and Scotland had done all that, and still they remained mere dilettantes. They lacked the advanced Irishman's professional respect for the deed." No cure, Brown added, "was as magical as a bold dramatic action. . . ."[15] Pearse appreciated this view better than any others of his time. His was to be the deed.

CONCLUSION

Had the three varieties of Irish Nationalism been combined in one, the four–part model of national development outlined in Chapter Three would have been complete: a sophisticated political organization mobilizing enormous political support, recognizing and cultivating a distinctive national culture, and inspiring to heroic deeds by the legends of the past. To some degree, of course, the three movements were intertwined. The Young Irelanders and some of the leaders of 1916—Pearse, for example—were both Revolutionary and Romantic Nationalists. Fenians and Gaelic Leaguers were able to vote for candidates of the Irish Party at general elections and the number of people thrilled by Fenian exploits went far beyond the formal membership of the I.R.B.

[14] Pearse, p. 125.
[15] Brown, p. 37.

Furthermore, until Parnell's death Constitutional Nationalism had operated with the support of violent people, and even in Redmond's day Irish members of Parliament who argued for moderation and home rule at Westminster often preached national independence and flirted with extremists in Ireland and America. Nevertheless, the fact remains that Irish Nationalism was divided. As a movement, Constitutional Nationalism was far removed from the visceral hatreds of the Fenians, and its concerns were more pragmatic and material than those of Romantic Nationalism. The Irish Party played no part in the cultural revival and was therefore divorced from some of the very best minds in Ireland, particularly among the young, who wanted more than simply a subordinate parliament in Dublin. As Oliver MacDonagh explains, "The orthodox Irish Nationalist of the 1880s and 1890s was scarcely aware that a 'problem' of anglicization existed."[16] Yet Constitutional Nationalism, shorn of the emotional power of its Land League days, and isolated from important currents of cultural change and revolutionary agitation in Ireland, still represented by far the strongest of the three movements in 1912. It was powerful, popular and successful. Its accomplishments included Catholic emancipation and land reform, and it appeared set for its final triumph—home rule. Romantic Nationalism had a relatively small following, and Revolutionary Nationalism was starved of both funds and followers. But what must be remembered is that revolutions are rarely made by mass movements; most of the people are spectators when guns begin to fire. Events finally conspired to rob the Constitutional Nationalists of their prize. In Chapters Six and Seven we shall see that their progress towards home rule was halted by Protestant resistence in 1914 and that this gave the revolutionaries the opportunity which they seized in 1916.

[16] Oliver MacDonagh, *Ireland* (Englewood Cliffs, N.J., 1968), p. 64.

5

America and the Irish Problem

THE IRISH AMERICANS

The Proclamation of the Irish Republic in 1916 spoke of Ireland's "exiled children in America." There was, and there remains, an American dimension to the Irish problem, and if we are to understand the Easter Rising, we have to know something about the Irish Americans. They were the ones who financed and sustained Irish Nationalism in the years before the Rising, and they were the ones who kept alive the dream of an independent Ireland when most at home would have settled for less.

The first Irish emigration to America was predominently Protestant. British policies in Ireland in the eighteenth century discriminated against nonconformist Protestants as well as Catholics. Many emigrated to religious freedom in America, where they became known as Scotch Irish—meaning presbyterians from Ulster. There were only thirty thousand Catholics in the American colonies in 1789, and in 1801 it was still possible for George Washington to tell the American people in his Farewell Address, "With slight shades of difference you have the same religion, manners, habits and political principles." By the mid–nineteenth century, however, the composition of the population began to change as immigrants from a variety of countries began to find in America a haven from political, religious, and economic distress. The first great wave of non-English immigrants was of Irish Catholics who fled Ireland from the time of the Great Famine in 1845. Within a few years they had made the Irish question almost as much an issue in American politics as it was in British politics.

Many of the prefamine Irish immigrants had been skilled artisans, tenant farmers and others who were not wretchedly poor. But then came the Great Famine of 1845 to 1851. Between 1845 and 1854 one and a half million Irish emigrated to the United States. These were the famine poor whom McCaffrey calls "refugees from disaster."[1] Huge numbers of them arrived destitute and became inhabitants of the urban, ethnic ghettos in the East. Their lives were grim and often criminal since ghetto problems of the past were similar to those of today. Later in the century, however, from 1870 or so, immigrants began to mirror improved living conditions in Ireland so that, taken as a whole, they proved to be a diverse group of people. The 1910 United States Census identified four and a half million residents who had been born in Ireland or were the children of at least one Irish-born parent. Millions more were second- or third-generation Americans who still considered themselves Irish. They provided hard labor for American industries and railroads, but some achieved economic and social prominence. By the turn of the century, they could be counted among the most successful people in America—railroad barons, justices of the New York Supreme Court, governors and congressmen. They were also supremely successful machine politicians, controlling major cities, such as Boston and New York. Not the least of their accomplishments were that they supported a rich and powerful Church and a large system of schools and colleges.

Irish-American Catholics remained resolutely Irish whereas Irish-American Protestants were quickly assimilated into the predominantly Anglo culture. Perhaps as many as fifteen American presidents could claim Irish ancestry, but only one Catholic, John

[1] Lawrence McCaffrey, *The Irish Diaspora in America* (Bloomington, Ind., 1976), chap. 4.

Kennedy, was popularly thought of as Irish. In an important sense, Irish Catholics had been forced to remain Irish. They were the victims of American nativism, an anti–Catholic, antiimmigrant hatred which mirrored the English nativism of the same period. In both America and England, Irish Catholics were disparaged in print and cartoon as drunkards, layabouts, thieves and apes. The Know–Nothing Party of the 1850s was anti–Irish, as were the American Protective Association and the populism of the 1880s and 1890s. The Irish were therefore forced to turn to each other for support. They joined a host of Irish social, fraternal, political, sporting, and benevolent societies. In addition, in the absence of the welfare state, the ghetto Irish were organized into potent voting blocs by machine Democratic politicians who discovered that by providing jobs and relief for the poor they could control the Irish vote. Finally, at the very heart—or perhaps soul—of the Irish–American community lay the Roman Catholic Church.

As a result of these social forces and affiliations, few Irish Americans were able, and few would have chosen, to live outside the Irish community. They lived and worshipped and played together, and they remembered together. And what they remembered was England's cruel repression of Ireland. In 1869, Irish–American author D. P. Conyngham issued a very solemn warning to England when he wrote, "How is it that the Government of England is so blind to the ruin that a people so numerous and powerful in foreign countries, and hating her so intensely, is sure to bring on her in her hour of troubles? It might be politic to try conciliation, instead of coercion, on such a people."[2] As Conyngham predicted, the Irish in America did work to "ruin" England. They did it in three ways. First, they sought to influence American foreign policy against England. Second, they supported the constitutional movement for home rule in Ireland. Third, they supported the revolutionary movement in Ireland that led to Easter Week, 1916, and a rebel-

[2] D. P. Conyngham, *The Irish Brigade and its Campaigns* (Boston, 1869), p. 81.

lion that came, as Conyngham had warned, during England's "hour of troubles."

IRISH AMERICANS AND AMERICAN FOREIGN POLICY

The Irish in America and the Irish in Ireland had different attitudes towards England, and the key to this difference lay in the phenomenon of Irish–American Nationalism. By the turn of the century the majority of Irish Americans had either been born in America or had left Ireland many years before. The Ireland they knew from experience or from tales told by parents and grandparents was impoverished and enslaved. They knew little of the land reforms of 1881, 1896 and 1903 or of the steadily improving Ireland of that time. Perhaps more than the Irish who had remained behind, Irish Americans passionately desired Ireland's liberation from English tyranny. In this respect, of course, they were *Irish* Nationalists. But they were also *Irish–American* Nationalists. Thomas Brown has shown that Irish–American Nationalism flourished as a response to the plight of the Ireland they had fled and their own problems as immigrants in America.[3] It was a response to the problems of economic hardship and nativist rejection in America. Irish Americans attributed their rejection in America to the improverished and enslaved condition of Ireland, and they reacted in two ways. First, they sought self–respect by working to liberate their homeland. Second, they sought acceptance in their adopted land by demonstrating that they were as loyal as the most loyal Americans. They expressed their patriotism in a fiercely anglophobic Americanism which managed to combine the cause of America with the cause of Ireland. They saw England as both the oppressor of Ireland and as the traditional enemy of American democracy. The net result was that it was easier for the Irish in America to plot the downfall of England than it was for the Irish in Ireland. There was an enormous difference between being Irish

[3] Thomas N. Brown, *Irish–American Nationalism, 1870–1890* (Philadelphia, 1966).

in Ireland and being Irish in America. As McCaffrey writes, "Irish nationalism jelled and flourished in the ghettos of urban America as a search for identity, an expression of vengeance, and a quest for respectability."[4]

It was this American component in Irish Nationalism which explains the determination of Irish Americans to work not only for Ireland's freedom but also for England's downfall, something few were planning in Ireland. For.example, John Mitchel, the Young Irelander who was rescued from an Australian convict settlement by an Irish–American expedition in 1853, pleaded Russia's case in his newspaper *The Citizen* during the Crimean War; and the Irish–American press supported Russia against England's ally, Japan, during the Russo–Japanese War of 1904 to 1905. During the Boer War in 1899 and 1900, Irish Americans led a powerful antiwar agitation with mass meetings throughout America, and they were largely responsible for the anti–British statements included in both the Democratic and Republican platforms in 1900. An Irish–American ambulance corps was sent to South Africa, where its members immediately abandoned medicine and took up arms. In 1897, 1904 and 1912, Anglo–American arbitration treaties were denounced by Irish Americans as alliances and were defeated in the Senate. Indeed, the Irish maintained a continuous attack on anything which might suggest Anglo–American friendship, and in 1907 German and Irish–American organizations began to work together in anticipation of a future European war.

In the years before World War I, the Irish acted as a critically important element in a number of coalitions — with antiimperialist Democrats, with senators determined to protect their foreign relations prerogatives against open–ended arbitration treaties, with German Americans, Russians, Boers and even nationalists in India. In every case the Irish–American interest was the same—to damage England. It was natural, therefore, that when World War I began, some Irish Americans supported the German cause and almost all the rest demanded that the United States maintain neu-

[4] McCaffrey, p. 107.

trality. As T. A. Bailey wrote, "From the outset it was clear that the American people would find it more than ordinarily difficult to avoid taking sides. This was a *world* war; and the United States, the historic asylum of the oppressed, contained a " 'menagerie of nationalists.' "[5] German and Irish Americans, for example, were just two of the communities that could not avoid taking sides in the war, and in October 1914, President Wilson confessed to the U.S. ambassador to England, "More and more, from day to day, the elements (I mean the several racial elements) of our population seem to grow restless and catch more and more the fever of the contest. We are trying to keep all possible spaces cool, and the only means by which we can do so is to make it demonstrably clear that we are doing everything that it is possible to do to define and defend neutral rights."[6] During the war, and particularly after the United States entered it in April 1917, President Wilson sent appeal after appeal to the United Kingdom government asking it to resolve the Irish question for the sake of Anglo–American harmony and the war effort.

IRISH AMERICANS AND CONSTITUTIONAL NATIONALISM

Irish–American Nationalism had an important effect on American politics and foreign policy, but it had an equally important impact on politics in the United Kingdom. When the leadership of the Irish Party was assumed by Parnell in 1880, he turned to America for financial support. At first, American funds went to fight the Irish Land War, but after the Irish Land Act of 1881 they were available to support Irish members of Parliament. Between 1880 and 1914 an almost continuous stream of Irish politicians visited the United States, as well as Australia and Canada, to raise

[5] Thomas A. Bailey, *A Diplomatic History of the American People* (New York, 1950), p. 610
[6] Alan J. Ward, *Ireland and Anglo–American Relations, 1899-1921* (London, 1969), p. 85.

money. Members of Parliament received no salaries until 1911, when annual payments of £400 were first made, but those Irish members who needed financial help received it, largely from American sources. Parnell himself went to America in 1880 and addressed a joint session of Congress, so important had the Irish question already become there. He returned with £20,000. John Redmond made American tours in 1883 (when he collected £15,000) and in 1886, 1895 and 1899. He returned from this last tour convinced that the split in the Irish Party caused by the Parnell divorce scandal in 1890 had seriously impaired the American fund–raising effort. The reunion of the party under his leadership in 1900 was brought about because of this diagnosis. Thereafter, Redmond and other leaders such as Joseph Devlin, John Dillon, William Redmond and T. P. O'Connor, returned regularly to gather funds in the United States and Canada. O'Connor visited America six times in all. In 1901 John Redmond formed the United Irish League of America which became an enormously successful auxiliary of the Irish Party. It sponsored large meetings in dozens of cities, its activities were widely reported in the press, and it raised very large sums of money, primarily for election and parliamentary expenses. F. S. L. Lyons estimates that fifty percent of the eighty or so Irish members received aid in the years 1900 to 1910 and that £70,000 ($350,000) was raised.[7] Contemporary accounts suggest that this estimate may be too low.

The success of Redmond's constitutional agitation in America was a damaging blow to those Irish Americans who favored a revolution in Ireland. Our earlier conclusion, however, that the Irish in America found it easier to work for England's downfall than did the Irish in Ireland was clearly demonstrated in 1914. In August of that year, as war broke out in Europe, John Redmond stood in the House of Commons to pledge Ireland's support to England in the war against Germany. Almost immediately the United Irish League collapsed in America and Redmond's leader-

[7] F. S. L. Lyons, *The Irish Parliamentary Party*, 1890–1910 (London, 1951), chap. 6.

ship was rejected by the American Irish. An interesting aspect of Redmond's campaign in America had been that the same crowds which came to cheer him could also be mobilized by the Clan na Gael, a revolutionary organization, to oppose England whenever Anglo–American relations appeared in danger of becoming too harmonious. But with the collapse of the United Irish League, the Clan came to monopolize the leadership of the Irish–American movement.

IRISH AMERICANS AND REVOLUTIONARY NATIONALISM

We have already seen in Chapter Four that there were very few active revolutionaries in Ireland in the twenty or thirty years before 1916. In large part this was due to the general improvements in Irish life and the political success of the home rule movement. The relative calm, however, also reflected the fact that England had driven out of Ireland several generations of revolutionaries, most of whom went to live in the United States. John Mitchel, for example, who had been transported to an Australian penal colony in 1848 for advocating revolution in the *United Irishman*, was rescued and brought to New York in 1853. Other Young Irelanders such as John O'Mahony and James Stephens fled to America, often via France, after their rebellion failed in 1848. Indeed, a nineteenth–century commentator wrote, "The result of the abortive insurrection of 1848 was to change the base of Irish revolution from Ireland to America."[8]

John Devoy, Jeremiah O'Donovan Rossa and a number of other revolutionaries arrived in America straight from British prisons in 1871 after the Fenian failures of the 1860s. Another revolutionary, Tom Clarke, who was to be executed for his part in the Easter Rising, first went to America in 1881 but was captured in England in 1883 on a Clan na Gael sabotage mission. He was imprisoned

[8] Philip H. Bagenal, *The American–Irish and their Influence on Irish Politics* (London, 1882), p. 111.

until 1898 and left again for America. By 1907, however, he was back in Dublin to reorganize the Irish Republican Brotherhood. He and all the others had used America as John Mitchel had declared he would use it when he arrived in 1853. "I mean," Mitchel had said, "to make use of the freedom guaranteed to me as a citizen . . . of America to help and stimulate the movement of European Democracy and especially of Irish independence."[9]

Irish revolutionaries in America supplied funds for the secret I.R.B. and formed the American auxiliary, the Fenian Brotherhood. By 1865 they numbered fifty thousand men, and British prisons were very soon loaded with Irish Americans arrested for treason or sedition on their return to Ireland or England. Many had participated in the Fenian rising of 1867 that was led by Thomas J. Kelly. Because a number of them were already naturalized citizens of the United States, they were the subjects of intense diplomatic pressure levied by the American government on their behalf. In 1867 and 1870 bands of Fenians invaded Canada, and in 1867 they sent the ship *Erin's Hope* to Ireland with supplies for the Fenian rising led by Kelly. The ship arrived too late, reflecting the Irish revolutionary art from 1798 to 1916.

The Fenian Brotherhood collapsed in the early 1870s, but another revolutionary organization, the Clan na Gael—founded in 1867 and now led by John Devoy—survived to carry the revolutionary cause into the twentieth century. The Clan supported the Land League agitation, but it never lost sight of revolution. One wing waged a campaign of bombing and terror in England from 1883 to 1885 that closely paralleled recent I.R.A. outrages. The Clan suffered from debilitating internal conflicts in the 1880s and 1890s, but it was revived in 1900 by John Devoy and Daniel Cohalan, an American–born lawyer and New York machine politician. Its members were still pledged to use physical force to liberate Ireland, but it committed no violent acts in the years before World War I. British consuls frequently saw Clan dynamiters in their

[9] Florence Gibson, *The Attitudes of the New York Irish Towards State and National Affairs, 1848–1892* (New York, 1951), p. 65.

dreams, but the organization actually concentrated on organizing the anti–English activities described earlier in this chapter. Ireland was not ready for revolution as even the most dedicated revolutionary could see. The Clan was dangerously weak by 1910, and the home rule movement had nearly destroyed the revolutionary impulse in Ireland. Devoy himself wrote: "From 1871 to 1916 [the I.R.B.] was maintained almost entirely by the moral and material support from the Clan na Gael. Envoys from the I.R.B. attended every Convention of the Clan na Gael and went back to carry on the work."[10]

Times were bad, but the Clan leaders did what they could while biding their time. They supported the nonrevolutionary Sinn Fein movement in its infancy because Sinn Fein opposed Redmond's Irish Party. The Clan regarded Constitutional Nationalism as a threat to eventual Irish independence and did anything it could to weaken its effect. The Clan's most important revolutionary act was to send Tom Clarke to Dublin to reorganize the almost extinct I.R.B. in 1907. From the cover of his tobacconist shop, Clarke waited for Ireland's opportunity. In New York, John Devoy also waited. He had never forgotten something he wrote in 1881: "If Ireland wins her freedom, she must wade to it through blood and suffering and sacrifice. . . . The people at home must be prepared—they must be armed. . . . We in America must do more than make speeches and subscribe money to keep the agitator alive! An agitation that must be fed and fostered and subsidized from abroad has nothing in it. Let us devote some of our spare cash to preparing Ireland for the final ordeal."[11]

CONCLUSION

The American connection was critically important for Irish Nationalism. It had, for example, helped the home rule movement to the brink of victory by 1914. Furthermore, British politicians were

[10] John Devoy, *Recollections of a Rebel* (New York, 1929), p. 392.
[11] Bagenal, p. 223.

well aware that Anglo–American relations would continue to suffer if the Irish question remained unresolved. For our purpose, however, the most significant American contribution was the revolutionary one. As Devoy had suggested, one faction of the Irish in America had worked to prepare Ireland for the final ordeal. Revolutionary Nationalism was terribly weak in 1914, but it was still alive and its moment was approaching.

6
Three Home Rule Bills and the Rise of Unionism

From the perspective of the Irish Republic, it would be natural to see the Easter Rising as the turning point in modern Irish history. It was, after all, the heroic act that ushered in the new state. But, from the broader perspective of Anglo–Irish relations, the turning point may have already occurred two years earlier when the Constitutional Nationalists had a great victory snatched from their grasp. The Third Home Rule Bill was about to become law in 1914 when it was blocked by the Protestants of Ulster using the threat of civil war. The Irish Party had played by the rules of the parliamentary game only to find that its opponents had broken those rules. World War I delayed the reckoning and provided a respite from one of the greatest constitutional crises in United Kingdom history, but it was a respite from which the constitutionalists never recovered.

Republicans were not inclined to see this defeat as a great loss for Ireland because home rule, a very limited measure of self-government, fell far short of their aspirations. They had always predicted that constitutionalism would fail because of English duplicity, and had it not failed they would have been denied their opportunity in 1916.

An appreciation of the Easter Rising, then, clearly hinges to a large degree on an appreciation of the events of 1914. Was there a genuine opportunity to settle the Irish problem in 1914 which was missed? Or was this simply a way station to the inevitable victory of Revolutionary Nationalism in 1916, the real turning point? In this chapter we will explore these questions.

We have already discussed in Chapter Three the evolution of Constitutional Nationalism and home rule in the nineteenth century. Its success can be measured by the fact that three home rule bills were introduced by the governments of Prime Minister Gladstone in 1886 and 1893 and that of Herbert Henry Asquith in 1912. Each of these Liberal governments depended on the votes of the Irish Party for its majority in the House of Commons and the price for Irish support was home rule.

The 1886 Home Rule Bill was defeated in the House of Commons when ninety–three Liberals deserted the government to vote with the Conservative opposition. The 1893 bill was approved in the House of Commons but was subsequently crushed in the House of Lords. However, the 1912 bill appeared certain of passage because the Parliament Act of 1911 deprived the Lords of their veto. Henceforward, they could only delay legislation for two years. If passed three times by the House of Commons in successive sessions, a bill would move on for the royal assent over the opposition of the Lords. This meant, of course, that the Home Rule Bill that Asquith introduced in April 1912 would have been implemented, on its third attempt, in 1914, had circumstances not conspired to rob the Constitutional Nationalists of their victory.

This sense that the Irish were robbed in 1914 has led historians to concentrate on the act of the Protestants' "robbery" rather than on what was stolen. The question of whether the home rule bills were good or bad has been neglected in part, no doubt, because the constitutional issues involved were very complex. We ought to ask, however, if the bills were really capable of finally settling the Irish problem.

HOME RULE AND THE CONSTITUTION

Home rule was a form of what is now known in Britain as "devolution," which is simply the process of creating subordinate regional parliaments to handle purely regional affairs. Legislative power is devolved to them. The Parliament at Westminster continues to legislate, first, for matters of concern to the whole United Kingdom, such as defence and foreign relations, and second, for those regions without their own parliaments.

The three home rule bills were nearly identical in their essential aspects. They proposed that a parliament be established in Dublin for Irish affairs. Ireland would have its own government, with ministers drawn from this parliament, and almost all of its domestic life would be in Irish hands, with the exception that no law could be passed to endow, establish or restrict religion. The United Kingdom Parliament would continue to legislate for the United Kingdom as a whole and for the regions without parliaments, England, Scotland and Wales.

Of course, no legislation of this kind could be absolutely perfect, but these home rule bills had a number of defects which would have made them very difficult to operate successfully. We should consider, very briefly, three particular flaws: the principle of representation, the constitutional relationship between the parliaments in Dublin and Westminster, and financial relations.

The Representation Dilemma

The representation flaw arose because of the two roles assigned to the Parliament at Westminster. It was to legislate both for the United Kingdom and for the regions without parliaments of their own. This meant that the Irish representatives at Westminster would have the right to participate not only in United Kingdom affairs, which was reasonable because they were still in the Union, but in English, Scottish and Welsh affairs, too, which was unreasonable.

This problem led Gladstone to propose in 1886 that the Irish should not sit at Westminster because it would be unfair for them to participate in English, Scottish and Welsh affairs while having a parliament of their own. But this meant that they would have no say at all in United Kingdom matters. Gladstone changed his mind in 1893 and agreed that they could sit at Westminster. But this simply reversed the problem. Now they could vote on United Kingdom matters, which was proper, but they could also vote on the affairs of the other regions, which was not. Furthermore, the Irish would have an important role in deciding which party would form the government. If the Liberal and Conservative parties were evenly balanced in the House of Commons, the eighty or so Irish members would actually decide not only which party would govern the United Kingdom but which party would govern England, Scotland and Wales, too.

Within the framework of Irish home rule, there really was no satisfactory resolution for this dilemma. If the Irish sat at Westminster they would be able to intervene in British affairs, but if they were denied seats they would be deprived of the right to participate in United Kingdom affairs. In 1912, therefore, Asquith offered an inelegant compromise. Ireland would have forty–two seats in the House of Commons, only half of the places the Irish population would have warranted. What this meant was that the Irish were to have fifty percent representation on United Kingdom matters which concerned them and the same fifty percent representation on British matters which did not!

Of course, the dilemma could have been resolved by giving home rule to England, Scotland and Wales, too, leaving the Westminster Parliament with no regional responsibilities at all, and Asquith appeared to endorse this in general terms when he introduced the Third Home Rule Bill in 1912. But the Liberals were themselves divided on the merits of additional regional parliaments, and there was no general demand for them. "Home rule all round," as it was called, was considered too heavy a price to pay to appease Irish Nationalists.

The representation dilemma arose because home rule was the response to a political crisis. Irish Nationalism clearly threatened the survival of the Union and the Irish Party was holding successive Liberal governments hostage. This was not true of any other region at that time so only Ireland was offered home rule. The object was to try to solve the Irish problem without altering the Constitution in any fundamental way, and, because of this, the home rule bills could always be attacked as political expedients. They were not attempts at coherent constitutional change.

The Constitutional Relationship

The representation issue aside, home rule also posed other constitutional problems. The most important of these was the vagueness of the proposed relationship between the two countries. In each bill, the United Kingdom parliament retained its legal supremacy. It could override the Dublin legislature, or even abolish home rule itself, by a simple act of Parliament. This meant that Ireland would always be at its mercy. Furthermore, through its "advice to the crown," which is constitutional language for the fact that the monarch has to do what the government advises, the royal veto could be used by the United Kingdom government to block Irish legislation.

The point at which the United Kingdom might intervene in one of these ways was never clear. The Liberals argued that Ireland would be protected by a "convention"—an unwritten constitutional rule—that intervention would only occur in some dire emergency. But after Northern Ireland received home rule in 1921, the United Kingdom regularly interfered in matters which had been devolved to Northern Ireland in circumstances which no one could call dire.

What this suggests is that the proposed relationship between Ireland and the United Kingdom was going to be extremely vague.

It had to depend on goodwill and trust—qualities notably lacking in the history of Anglo–Irish relations. The opponents of home rule, Conservatives and Irish Protestants, certainly did not trust Irish Nationalists. They believed that an Irish parliament would be used as a stepping stone to independence, and they could not imagine that a Liberal government—certainly one supported by Irish votes at Westminister—would have the courage to overrule Dublin. Some of them argued that there was an equal danger. If a United Kingdom government intervened too much in Irish affairs, it would surely provoke the Irish into demanding full independence. Neither the home rule bills nor the unwritten constitution of the United Kingdom provided guidelines or guarantees concerning the proposed relationship between Dublin and Westminster. The Irish would be extremely sensitive to any apparent invasion of their autonomy, and the United Kingdom would see any Irish demand for increased authority as a prelude to independence.

The Financial Relationship

Many critics of home rule believed that a conflict between the two political systems would arise from an invasion of Protestant religious rights by a Catholic–dominated parliament in Dublin. Religious freedom was guaranteed, however, in the home rule bills themselves, and the more probable source of conflict would have been the proposed financial relationship between Ireland and the United Kingdom. The home rule bills all gave the Irish Parliament responsibility for Irish domestic legislation but left control of the important taxes with the United Kingdom. There was always to be a distinction, then, between the Parliament raising money for Irish affairs at Westminster, and the Parliament spending these revenues in Dublin. Irish domestic programs would be at the mercy of taxing policies set at Westminster. It was ominous for the future that the Irish Party always believed the financial terms would have to be renegotiated. John Redmond, for example, accepted the third

Home Rule Bill as a "final settlement" but added, "Admittedly it is a provisional settlement. . . . When the time for revision does come . . . we will be entitled to complete power for Ireland over the whole of our financial system."[1]

The opponents of home rule attacked these three constitutional flaws in every one of the many debates on home rule over a period of nearly thirty years. Their major concern was not to improve the legislation, because they wanted to defeat home rule altogether, but this does not mean that their criticisms were unsound. We must not allow sympathy for the Nationalists to obscure the fact that the home rule bills were not particularly good pieces of legislation. Furthermore, we cannot accept uncritically the view that the Irish Party would have settled for these terms in the long run. But whether good or bad, home rule for a united Ireland was not to be. The success of the home rule agitation brought about its own downfall. It provoked a Protestant backlash.

PROTESTANT NATIONALISM: THE UNIONIST RESPONSE TO HOME RULE

In purely constitutional terms, the simplest remedy for Irish Nationalism would have been to abandon the Union and give Ireland its independence, as O'Connell's repeal movement had demanded in the 1840s. This would have avoided the constitutional anomalies inherent in home rule, but it was impossible in the nineteenth century when every member of the House of Commons who was not an Irish Nationalist believed that an Irish settlement had to satisfy three conditions. First, it had to protect the Union. Ireland could not be allowed to secede. Second, having regard to the troubled religious history of Ireland, it had to protect the religious rights of the Protestant minority. Third, it had to recognize the constitutional supremacy of the United Kingdom so that, if faced with Nationalist demands for more powers or with threats

[1] R. J. Lawrence, *The Government of Northern Ireland: Public Finance and Public Services*, 1921–1964 *(Oxford, 1965)*, p. 189.

to Protestant religious freedom, the United Kingdom could over-rule the Irish Parliament or even abolish it.

The Liberals and Conservatives agreed on these three conditions, and it was only by working within this framework that the Irish Party could hope to win any support in Britain for a measure of self–government. This is why O'Connell's demand for repeal was abandoned by the Constitutional Nationalists in the 1870s. Under Gladstone's leadership, the Liberals came to believe that it was possible to devise a home rule bill which would satisfy the conditions, but the Conservatives were convinced that it was impossible.

The First Home Rule Bill in 1886 created the alliance which was, in the end, to defeat Constitutional Nationalism. It included the predominantly Anglican landlord class, many of them living in England, who believed that an Irish Parliament would rob them of their property through expropriation or a disadvantageous land reform. It included die–hard Tories, many in Parliament and the army, who believed that Irish home rule would be the first step in the disintegration of the British Empire. As Ireland went, they argued, so would go Egypt, India, South Africa and the rest. It included, of course, the predominantly Presbyterian Protestants of Ulster who believed that a Parliament in Dublin, dominated by Catholics, would be controlled from Rome. This group included both the urban working class, which had frequently participated in religious riots in Belfast and other northern cities in the nineteenth century, and the Orange Society which, with its many lodges, provided the grass roots organization for the movement. Finally, it included the Conservative Party.

From about 1886, this whole ensemble was known as "Unionists," although the term concealed some important distinctions. For example, there was a considerable difference between Southern and Northern Irish Unionists. The former were distinguished by their Anglicanism, their ownership of land and their status as an elite. They were a small minority of less than ten percent in a population of Catholics. The Northern, or Ulster, Unionists included Anglicans, Presbyterians and a smaller number of Methodists and represented every kind of occupation and social class. They were about half the population in the nine counties of Ulster and about two thirds in the area finally identified as Northern Ireland in 1921. The solid core of the Unionists' resistance to home rule naturally lay in the North. As Patrick Buckland noted, "Ulster Protestants felt that they had little in common with either the Catholic majority or the scattered and largely landed Protestant minority in the agricultural South. This feeling created the Ulster question and Ulster unionism." Furthermore, there was virtually no dialogue between the Unionists and Nationalists—only, as Buckland describes it, "mutual recrimination in slanging matches undertaken with a view to influencing opinion in Great Britain."[2]

The Unionists in Ireland had decided to fight, and as the home rule movement gained in strength so did they. Gladstone could insist that home rule posed no threat to the Protestant community because the Dublin Parliament would be constitutionally subordinate to Westminster, but the Unionists did not believe him. What was at stake, they believed, was the union with Britain that protected the Empire, their land, their religion and their status. Conservative politicians in Britain shared the Irish Protestants' antipathy to home rule, but they also used it as a weapon against Liberal governments. To restore Conservative fortunes, Lord Churchill had advised in 1885, "the Orange card" was the one to play. He added later, "Ulster will fight and Ulster will be right."[3] The words "Conservative" and "Unionist" quickly became synonymous.

The 1886 Home Rule Bill was defeated in the House of Commons and the 1893 bill was defeated in the House of Lords. Indeed, it was clear that the very large Conservative majority in the Lords would veto home rule indefinitely. But then the Liberals changed the rules—they destroyed the veto. The 1906 general election had

---

[2] Patrick Buckland, *Irish Unionism Two: Ulster Unionism and the Origins of Northern Ireland, 1886–1922* (Dublin, 1973), p. xxix, xxxv.
[3] Robert Kee, *The Green Flag* (New York, 1972), pp. 400–401.

returned the Liberals to office—for the first time since 1894—with a very large majority, which freed them from their old dependence on the Irish Party. Home rule was therefore put aside and the Irish Party was offered only a very weak measure of devolution in 1907, which it rejected. In 1909, however, the House of Lords provoked a constitutional crisis by rejecting the Liberals' budget, which contained a number of social reforms. Two elections were subsequently fought, in January and December 1910, both of which produced Liberal governments that were dependent on the Irish Party. Two things followed. First, in 1911 the government forced the Conservative Lords to accept the Parliament Act, which, as we have already seen, limited the lords' veto to only two years. They did this by threatening that they would create enough Liberal peers to outnumber the Conservatives. Second, in April 1912, the government introduced the Third Home Rule Bill for their Irish allies. Since the lords could no longer obstruct the measure indefinitely, it was clear that home rule would become law in 1914 at its third attempt. It was this fact which caused the Unionists to prepare for their last stand.

The Unionists were now faced with certain defeat, ironically, after several decades of beneficial legislation in Ireland. The Conservative governments of Lord Salisbury (1895–1902) and Arthur Balfour (1902–1905) and the Liberal governments of Sir Henry Campbell–Bannerman (1905–1908) and Herbert Henry Asquith (1908–1916) had introduced a number of reforms which resolved many of Ireland's material grievances. These included local government reform in 1898, the Department of Agriculture and Technical Instruction for Ireland in 1899 and a Catholic University in 1908. The most important measure was the Land Act of 1903 which, with a 1909 amendment, enabled two hundred thousand Irish farmers to buy the land they farmed. The Unionists, measuring Ireland's problems in material terms, believed that an Irish parliament was even less necessary than before, and they found it hard to accept that Constitutional Nationalism was as strong as ever.

The arguments used against home rule by the Unionists in 1886 and 1893 now took on a new urgency. The constitutional weaknesses and dangers inherent in home rule were identified again. The Irish Party was accused of being separatist in disguise. It would simply use home rule as a step towards full independence. Unionists even used John Redmond's own words to condemn him. In the United States in 1910, he had said, "[Home rule] concessions are only valuable because they strengthen the arms of the Irish people to push on to the great goal of independence."[4] Redmond tried to counter this by insisting, "We want peace with [England] and we deny we are separatists. We say we are willing, as Parnell was willing, to accept a subordinate Parliament created by statute of this Imperial Legislature as a final settlement of Ireland's claim."[5] But the Unionists simply did not believe him and they recalled an argument used by Joseph Chamberlain and Arthur Balfour in 1893 that no genuine Nationalist could accept such a limited measure of home rule as a "final settlement." Balfour repeated that only full independence would satisfy an authentic Nationalist. Either Redmond was lying when he said he would accept home rule or he did not represent a true Nationalist movement. Balfour did not believe that the Irish people really wanted independence and that, given time, the reforms of recent years would produce a completely loyal Ireland without home rule.[6] The Irish might retain a distinctive cultural identity, as had the Scots, but they would not want political independence.

Even if it was true that Irish Nationalism as represented by the Irish Party was genuine, the Unionists still had a most impressive argument in their repertoire. Ireland, they argued, was not a single nation or race. It was two nations, and Redmond represented only one. If the Catholics were entitled to self–determination, so were the Protestants. Chamberlain had made this point in the House of

[4] Ian Malcolm, "Home Rule All Round," *Nineteenth Century*, v. 68, Nov. 1910, pp. 791–799.
[5] London *Times*, 12 April 1912, p. 14.
[6] Arthur Balfour, *Nationality and Home Rule* (London, 1914).

Commons in 1886—to a chorus of Irish denials—and it was often repeated after 1912. By then, of course, Catholic Nationalism had become even less acceptable to the Protestants because it was increasingly being defined in exclusively Gaelic terms by Romantic Nationalists. The Protestants certainly did not believe they belonged to that Irish nation. The Irish Party tried to counter this argument and John Redmond, for example, replied, "The two-nation theory is to us an abomination and a blasphemy."[7] Ireland, he insisted, was one nation, not two. But although the two-nation theory was not well articulated in the debates on home rule, it was fundamental to the Unionist position. One of the important effects of the recent crisis in Northern Ireland had been the widespread recognition, at last, that Ireland does contain two nations—or at least two quite distinct political and cultural communities—which can only be brought together gradually, if at all, and by their mutual consent.

The arguments for and against home rule had changed little since 1886 and 1893, but in 1912 the Unionists changed their tactics. Their dissent became rebellion. They had always said that they would use force rather than accept home rule, but they did not carry out this threat until the House of Lords lost its veto power in 1911. Bonar Law, who had become leader of the Conservative Party in 1911, was particularly important in this campaign. Addressing a mass meeting at Blenheim Palace in 1912, he said "I can imagine no length of resistence to which Ulster can go in which I should not be prepared to support them, and in which, in my belief, they would not be supported by the overwhelming majority of the British people."[8]

Law and his colleagues justified their support for rebellion by insisting that they were upholding, not attacking, the constitution. In their view, the Act of Union of 1800 was a fundamental constitutional document which the government could not amend with-

[7] Denis R. Gwynn, *The History of Partition, 1912–1925* (Dublin, 1950), p. 64.
[8] Robert Blake, *Unrepentent Tory* (New York, 1956), p. 130.

out a clear mandate from the people. The act had stated that Ireland and Britain would be governed by a single parliament. Home rule broke this solemn promise by removing all Irish legislation to the Irish Parliament in Dublin. Law said that he was prepared to accept the verdict of a general election on the issue. The Liberals replied that the Union would be unimpaired by home rule because the Irish Parliament would be subordinate to a United Kingdom Parliament in which the Irish would be represented. They rejected a general election because it would be fought on many issues and would therefore not resolve the issue of a home rule mandate one way or the other.

The Conservatives' constitutional reasoning was rather shaky, if only because it appeared to deny parliamentary sovereignty—the principle that Parliament can amend or abridge any law, including the Act of Union—but it was used, nonetheless, to condone a rebellion. How was that rebellion planned? Sir Edward Carson, a member of Parliament for Dublin University and not an Ulsterman himself, accepted the leadership of the Ulster Unionists in the summer of 1911. Under his leadership, they prepared their resistence. The Ulster Unionist Council, which had been formed in 1905, became the hub of the movement. In September 1911, they decided to prepare for a provisional government which would take control of Ulster if home rule became law. On September 18, 1912, almost five hundred thousand people, including virtually all of the adult Protestants in Ireland, signed the Ulster Covenant in which they pledged to oppose home rule by force.

In January 1913, the Ulster Volunteer Force was formed and in March 1914, in what has been called the Curragh Mutiny, the officers of the Curragh army base, west of Dublin, declared that they would resign their commissions rather than be ordered to Ulster to put down a Protestant rebellion. Finally, in April 1914, about twenty thousand rifles were smuggled into Ireland from Germany by the Ulster Volunteers in the Larne gunrunning. Colvin described the situation these events created in Ireland in his biography of Carson: "If we consider these two groups of events of the Curragh and Larne in March and April 1914, it will be seen that before them the British Government was armed and the Loyalists of Ulster were unarmed, and that after them the British Government was disarmed and the Ulster Loyalists were armed."[9] The government did consider the arrest of the Unionist leaders, the "Ulster rabble" as they were called in the Cabinet,[10] for these flagrantly illegal acts but rejected the idea for fear of provoking a violent response in Ulster.

Dangerfield has argued recently that the Liberal government could have put down this incipient Ulster rebellion without great difficulty had it shown the courage to act. The Ulster Covenant, he says, "was no great threat. It committed them, at most, to a state of mind."[11] But no one expected nearly half a million men and women to take up arms. A large number of Unionists, however, were prepared to fight for Ulster Protestantism and the extremely efficient Larne gunrunning provided them with more than enough arms. Ireland was, indeed, on the verge of a Unionist–inspired civil war.

These Unionist preparations had not gone unnoticed by Irish Nationalists. As we saw in Chapter Four, Revolutionary Nationalists were instrumental in organizing a counterforce, the Irish National Volunteers, in Dublin in November 1913. They were badly underfinanced, unlike the Ulster Volunteers who had the wealth of industrial Belfast and Conservative England behind them, but in May 1914, they were able to import nine hundred old rifles from Germany in the gunrunning at Howth, outside Dublin, and a further six hundred in August at Kilcoole in County Wicklow. The Unionists could certainly out–gun the Nationalists, but the significance of these antiquated weapons was that they finally saw service in Dublin in the Easter Rising. Ironically, the gunrunning was undertaken by sympathetic Protestant home rulers, not Revo-

[9] Ian Colvin, *Carson the Statesman* (New York, 1935), p. 376.
[10] Alan J. Ward, *Ireland and Anglo–American Relations, 1899–1921* (London, 1969), p. 40.
[11] George Dangerfield, *The Damnable Question* (Boston, 1976), p. 76.

lutionary Nationalists, and many were serving in World War I when the Rising broke out.

John Redmond saw the growth of the National Volunteers as a threat to the authority of the Irish Party, and he forced a number of his nominees onto the committee of the organization with an ultimatum in June 1914. However, the I.R.B. remained in secret control.

By the summer of 1914, then, there were two rival mass movements in Ireland, both with private armies: one determined to see that home rule would be enforced and the other determined to see that it would not. Approximately one hundred thousand National Volunteers stood opposite the same number of Ulster Volunteers who had a distinct advantage in weapons. Whether the Unionists were or were not bluffing is still being debated, but the evidence is overwhelming that the probability of a civil war in Ireland was extremely high. We simply cannot ignore the Ulster Volunteers, the Larne gunrunning, the Ulster Covenant, the predispositions of army officers, an enormous number of whom were born in Ulster, the value of the Conservative support, or the siege mentality of the time. It was an incendiary situation, and in July 1914 the Army Council advised the government that a civil war in Ireland would tie up the entire British Expeditionary Force—the army kept in reserve in Britain for possible crises aboard—which would jeopardize the security of the British Empire.[12]

THE POLITICAL CRISIS OF 1914

As the two sides prepared themselves in Ireland, the Home Rule Bill proceeded on its way through Parliament. The government never seemed to have accepted that civil war was really imminent in Ulster. Asquith, for example, argued that the North was bluffing and that the greater danger was of a Nationalist–inspired war if home rule were denied. Nevertheless, he opened secret discussions with both sides late in 1913 to try to secure a settlement to which

[12] Ward, p. 265.

both could consent. At the heart of these discussions was the notion that Ireland should be partitioned, if only for a short time, into two parts.

It was the Unionist leaders, Carson and Law, who first suggested partition, although it clearly implied the sacrifice of the Southern Unionists to the home rule parliament. They proposed that all nine Ulster counties might be excluded from home rule, leaving only twenty-three to be represented in the Dublin Parliament. They later amended this to six counties because three of the nine—Donegal, Monaghan and Cavan—had large Catholic majorities. Indeed, in the nine counties as a whole, there was a small Catholic majority and the Irish Nationalists held one more seat in Parliament than the Unionists. The six counties still included two, however—Fermanagh and Tyrone—with small Catholic majorities. The core of the Protestant strength lay in the city of Belfast and the four counties of the northeast: Armagh, Antrim, Down, and Derry.

Informal negotiations continued until July 21, 1914, when at the suggestion of King George V, the Buckingham Palace Conference was convened in a final attempt to secure an agreement. By then, the issue of partition had been refined into two formulas. The government and the Irish Party proposed that six counties should be temporarily excluded from home rule for a period of six years, after which time they would be included automatically. This proposal contained an implied concession which was extremely important. At some point during the six years a general election would have to be called. If the Conservatives won, they would have an opportunity to amend home rule to the satisfaction of the Unionists. This means that Redmond had opened the door just a little to the possibility of permanent exclusion for some part of Ulster. The Unionists, however, rejected the proposal. They insisted that temporary exclusion was simply a stay of execution. Furthermore, for two reasons they were not prepared to gamble on the possibility of a Conservative election victory. First, the Conservatives might lose. Second, the decision as to whether they would go into the Dublin Parliament should be made by the people of Ulster, not the United Kingdom electorate as a whole.

The Unionists countered by proposing that the six counties be permanently excluded unless they chose on a county–by–county basis to accept home rule. This, too, contained an implied concession, because if the six counties voted for or against home rule on the basis of their religious preferences the two with small Catholic majorities might choose home rule. This would reduce the excluded area to only four counties, the solid Protestant heartland.

Redmond may have opened the door to permanent exclusion in his acceptance of temporary exclusion, but we do not know if he could have carried his party with him. The public position of the Irish Party was that the permanent exclusion of any part of Ireland from home rule was unacceptable. It would mean recognizing the existence of two nations, denying the principle of majority rule for the island as a whole, and violating the unity of the Irish economy. Furthermore, there were large pockets of Catholics even in Belfast and the four predominantly Protestant counties. No matter what area was excluded, there would always be the problem of a Catholic minority, which no partition plan could completely solve.

Similarly, we do not know if Carson and Law could have carried their supporters. Partition meant accepting home rule for most of Ireland, with dire consequences predicted for the future of property and the British Empire. And most important, it meant sacrificing the Southern Unionists who had an enormous amount of support in the Conservative Party.

The obstacles to partition were immense, but it seems obvious that some form of partition would have been preferable to a civil war initiated by the Unionists, if this was, indeed, what Ireland faced. The exclusion of four counties, with some additional border adjustments, might have minimally satisfied the Unionists' demand for exclusion without being in violation of home rule enough to justify a Nationalist civil war. The excluded area would have included a substantial Catholic minority, but it could have been protected by the United Kingdom Parliament and by explicit guarantees of religious freedom. This proposal could only have come from the Asquith government because neither the Irish Party, who publicly claimed the whole of Ireland, nor the Unionists, who either opposed home rule or claimed the whole of Ulster, could make the first move. We have no assurance that such a plan would have been acceptable to, or could have been forced upon, the two sides, but the issue is moot because the government did not make the offer. There is some evidence that Asquith was considering an amendment to the Home Rule Bill in late July to permanently exclude six counties, but World War I intervened. Dangerfield argues that exclusion would have been "unheroic, indeed perfidious," but such a judgement must assume that the Unionists had no case for special consideration and posed no serious threat to public order.[13] Both assumptions are wrong.

The collapse of the Buckingham Palace Conference on July 24, 1914, left the Home Rule Bill essentially in its form as introduced in 1912. It had passed through the House of Commons on May 25 and had gone on to the House of Lords for the last time. There, on June 23, the government proposed an amendment to temporarily exclude six counties. This was rejected by the Lords who substituted an outrageous amendment that the whole of Ulster—all nine counties—be permanently excluded. When the government refused to accept this change, the bill was finally approved, as originally framed, over the objections of the Lords, and it received the royal assent on September 14. Home rule for a united, thirty-two county Ireland was now on the statute books. The United Kingdom, however, had been at war since August 4, and the passage of home rule was immediately followed by a suspensory act that delayed its implementation for the duration of the war. The Unionists accepted this arrangement in the interest of prosecuting the war, but they did not intend to give up their fight. Home rule was now law, but the Unionists had no intention of accepting this as final.

---

[13] Dangerfield, p. 118.

CONCLUSION

A turning point had been reached, then, in the summer of 1914. The conventional view is that a choice had to be made at that time between home rule or no home rule for the whole of Ireland. There are many people who still argue that, had the government "called Ulster's bluff," the Unionists would have abandoned their protest and accepted the inevitable home rule. They also argue that home rule would have solved the Irish problem. It would have been, as Redmond had promised, a "final settlement." Each of these conclusions, however, is suspect.

First, as we have seen, by 1914 the real choice for Ireland was not between home rule for a united Ireland and continuation of the Union but between civil war and a plan of exclusion for the Protestants of the North. Second, the weight of the evidence is that Ulster was not bluffing. Home rule could not have been imposed on a united Ireland without an explosion. Third, in the long run it is doubtful that home rule would have ended the Irish problem. It was not only Revolutionary and Romantic Nationalists who did not accept it as final; many Constitutional Nationalists themselves wanted full independence and saw home rule as a means to that end, not an end in itself. Furthermore, the home rule bills were flawed and would have exacerbated any conflicts over their respective powers between Ireland and the United Kingdom, thereby provoking Irish demands for full independence. Even the evident willingness of the Irish Party to accept bills which gave them less financial power than they believed necessary is suspicious because it suggests that they were accepting home rule simply in order to gain a foothold on Irish independence.

The real turning point for Ireland, then, may well have been not the failure of home rule but the failure of the Liberal government to devise and impose a plan of partition in 1914. The significance of this missed opportunity must not be underestimated. Carson, the undisputed leader of the Ulster Unionists, and Law, the leader of the Conservative Party, believed with other Unionists that the constitutional imperfections of home rule contained the seeds of future discord between Ireland and the United Kingdom. They also believed that the home rule movement was a disguised separatist movement which would take advantage of any discord to move towards Irish independence. They must have known that home rule might not be final. By accepting home rule with partition, therefore, they were accepting the possibility of an independent Ireland in the South. By insisting on partition, they were trying to ensure that if or when this came about, the Protestant population of the North would be protected by being excluded. When this is considered in association with the fact that the leaders of the Irish Party, by accepting temporary exclusion for six counties, had opened the door to permanent exclusion for the North, it becomes clear that the solution of the Irish problem may well have been close at hand in 1914. It was a home rule settlement, for either twenty–six or twenty–eight counties, which would have contained the potential for further progress towards Irish independence because the problem of the Ulster Protestants would have been solved. This formula was not adopted until 1920, but by then it was too late. The Revolutionary Nationalists had already seized their opportunity in 1916.

7

World War I: England's Weakness and Ireland's Opportunity

CONSTITUTIONAL NATIONALISM AND THE WAR

On the day before the United Kingdom entered World War I, John Redmond stood in the House of Commons to pledge Ireland's support. This was a dramatic gesture because for seven hundred and fifty years it had been thought that Ireland posed a threat to Britain's security. Henry II had feared the growth of a Norman state in Ireland, and the Tudor conquest had been intended, in large part, to secure the country from England's enemies. During the reign of Elizabeth I, Irish rebels received aid several times from Spain and in 1690, seven thousand French troops landed to support James II against William of Orange. In December 1796, fourteen thousand French soldiers sailed from Brest to support the United Irishmen, but were unable to land. A smaller expedition with about eleven hundred men did land in County Mayo in August 1798, and another French expedition was intercepted by the British navy in October 1798.

These were distant events but strong memories, reinforced by the more recent endorsement of the Boer cause by Irish Nationalists during the Boer War of 1899 to 1902. In 1901, Lord Salisbury, the British prime minister, had declared: "We know now from our South African experiences the danger of letting Ireland have a measure of independence. We know now that if we allowed those who are leading Irish politics unlimited power of making preparations against us, we should have to begin by conquering Ireland, if ever we had to fight any other power."[1] Redmond quickly moved to allay these fears in August 1914, and the foreign secretary, Sir Edward Grey, admitted that "the one bright spot in the very dreadful situation is Ireland."[2] John Redmond followed his speech in the House of Commons with a recruiting campaign in Ireland where, with very few exceptions, both Nationalists and Unionists supported the war. Indeed, in America, the old Fenian, Devoy, bemoaned the "almost universal approval of John's pledge . . . . The moral rottenness at home is the worst part of it."[3]

Few Irish Americans were as revolutionary as Devoy and few were very actively pro–German, but the first year of the war illustrated the considerable difference between the Irish in Ireland and the Irish in America. By August 1915, for example, there were 132,454 Irishmen in the British Army, including 77,511 Catholics and 52,943 Protestants. More than eighty–one thousand had volunteered since the war began. By April 1916, the total had reached 150,183, compared to fifteen hundred or so republicans who turned out for the Rising. There was no doubt, then, that the moderation of the Constitutional Nationalists was approved by the majority of the Irish people. In America, however, Redmond's support for the war led to the almost total collapse of the United Irish League, the organization he had led so successfully for fourteen years. By 1915 he was maintaining the organization with funds sent from Ireland—a stunning reversal of the prewar pattern of financial support.

By endorsing the war, Redmond had certainly not rejected Irish Nationalism, although Irish Americans assumed he had. In fact, neither the Nationalists nor the Unionists were willing to disband

[1] Alan J. Ward, *Ireland and Anglo–American Relations, 1899–1921* (London, 1969), pp. 265–266.
[2] Robert Kee, *The Green Flag* (New York, 1972). p. 515.
[3] Ward, p. 102.

their volunteer organizations during what they anticipated would be a short war. When it was over, the Nationalists intended to ensure that home rule would be implemented as approved in 1914, and the Unionists were equally determined to ensure that it would not, or certainly not without excluding the north. The Nationalists were particularly buoyant because the royal assent was given to home rule on September 14. It was suspended for the duration of the war, of course, but Nationalists now believed they held the advantage and that their unqualified loyalty during the war could only strengthen their claim. As Redmond said in July 1915: "Given these two things—Ireland doing her duty to herself in the war and Ireland doing her duty to herself in keeping her political and military organizations intact. . .there is nothing more certain in this world than that as soon as the war ends Ireland will enter into the enjoyment of her inheritance."[4] But the longer the war lasted, the weaker Redmond's position was to become.

As the war lengthened, the Constitutional Nationalists suffered four major setbacks. First, the Irish National Volunteers split in September 1914, with about twelve thousand reorganizing as the Irish Volunteers in October 1914 under the leadership of Professor Eoin MacNeill. They believed that only a self–governing Ireland should participate in the war. The majority—about one hundred sixty thousand—were renamed the National Volunteers and remained loyal to Redmond. The Ulster Volunteers and National Volunteers, however, both began to suffer erosion from the effects of British recruitment in 1915; whereas the Irish Volunteers did not, even growing to about sixteen thousand by April 1916. In August 1915 they showed their strength by organizing a funeral in Dublin for an old Fenian, O'Donovan Rossa, who had died in America. By their design the funeral became a great demonstration for Irish independence.

Second, the Unionists strengthened their position by joining the coalition government which Prime Minister Asquith formed in 1915. Redmond refused to join, but Sir Edward Carson became

[4] Kee, p. 526.

attorney general, and when he resigned in October he was succeeded by his militant Unionist colleague, Sir F. E. Smith. Fierce opponents of home rule were now inside the government.

Third, the government had no intention of entrusting Irish home defence to the rival National and Ulster Volunteers, a suggestion offered by Redmond in the House of Commons on August 3. Indeed, the War Office was particularly unresponsive to recognizing the Nationalists' identity in any official way. Although there was an Ulster division in the army, the south of Ireland was denied a division with any specifically Nationalist character, such as badges or insignia.

Fourth, the longer the war continued, with its heavy toll of lives in France, the more necessary military conscription became. In any war, there are large numbers of people who would rather not serve in the armed forces—for whatever reason—and in Ireland the threat of conscription had the effect of encouraging membership in the Irish volunteers, the antiwar organization. The Irish were omitted from the general conscription program of 1916, and again in 1918, because the government did not want to provoke or encourage extremism. But the threat always loomed over Ireland.

REVOLUTIONARY NATIONALISM AND THE WAR

Constitutional Nationalism ultimately suffered from the war, but Revolutionary Nationalism was slow to benefit. The Irish prospered economically from food exports and job opportunities, and the majority of the Catholic population certainly supported Redmond. Indeed, Ireland might well have emerged from even a long war without an internal crisis had it not been for the activities of Revolutionary Nationalists, members of the Irish Republican Brotherhood, who had penetrated the leadership of the new Irish Volunteers.

When war was declared, the revolutionary I.R.B. Supreme Council resolved "to work for an insurrection in arms against

England to be launched at the earliest possible moment, without further provocation by England than her continued government of Ireland, and the military occupation of Ireland by an English garrison."[5] This was the position of the leadership of the Clan na Gael in the United States, too, but it was not yet the official position of the Irish Volunteers. Their leader, Eoin MacNeill, believed that the organization should be maintained to protect home rule, not to prepare for revolution. On the headquarters staff of the Volunteers, however, were three men—Patrick Pearse, director of military organization; Thomas MacDonagh, director of military training; and Joseph Plunkett, director of military operations—who were members of the I.R.B. and were secretly plotting to lead the Volunteers into an insurrection. In the summer of 1915, for example, Plunkett made his way to Berlin by way of New York to request help from the German government. None of this was known to MacNeill, the chairman of the Irish Volunteer executive and chief of staff, nor to two other members of the headquarters staff, Blumer Hobson, the quartermaster, and The O'Rahilly, the director of arms. This was an absurdly clumsy arrangement for which the rebels were to pay heavily in 1916, but without this deceit, there would have been no Rising at all.

The leaders of the Clan na Gael in America had already begun to cooperate with the Germans on two levels as soon as the war began. They openly cooperated with German–American organizations to oppose any American support for Britain and they secretly negotiated with Ambassador Bernstorff and other German diplomats to secure support for an insurrection in Ireland. They served as liaison between the rebels in Ireland and the German government.

Sir Roger Casement was in the United States soliciting funds for the National Volunteers, before the division in its ranks, when the war broke out. He immediately saw an opportunity to implement plans for Germany to support Irish independence, which he had promoted in pamphlets before the war. It was he who drafted a

[5] Ward, p.79.

declaration of Irish–American support for Germany which was signed by the Clan na Gael executive in August 1914, and he and John Devoy met with Ambassador Bernstorff to broach the idea of an Irish brigade which could be formed from Irish prisoners of war in Germany. Financed by the Clan, Casement left New York for Berlin in October 1914, and in November secured a German declaration of support for Irish independence. On December 28, Germany signed an agreement to equip an Irish brigade which would be sent to fight in Ireland, with supporting German officers and men, if Germany should win a victory at sea. In actuality, however, Casement's plan was a disaster because only fifty–five prisoners, of rather poor military quality, volunteered for the brigade.

Casement was an expensive ally for the Clan na Gael, which spent $10,000 on his mission from its very limited resources. John Devoy tells of sending $100,000 to Ireland during this period, but this was an exaggeration because he was worried by the shortage of money and resented Casement's drain on the Clan's resources.[6] The sum sent was probably less than half that amount. Whatever the American contribution may have been to the Rising, it was the only outside financial contribution of any signficance because there is no evidence that any German money was sent to Ireland. The most important problem for the revolutionaries, however, was less the shortage of money than the indifference of the Irish towards revolution. The Revolutionary Nationalists were making progress in 1915, but hardly enough to encourage thoughts of a rising which had any chance of military success.

The Irish Volunteers and the miniscule Irish Citizen Army, which had been organized by the Irish Transport and General Workers' Union during a violent Dublin transport strike in 1913, paraded and carried out maneuvers quite publicly, protected by the chief secretary's desire to avoid a confrontation or crisis in Ireland. There was also a steady stream of antiwar publications, one succeeding another as they were banned, and the government was finding it extremely difficult to secure convictions of those

[6] Ward, pp. 72 and 78.

arrested for antiwar activities from Irish juries. But no one would have said an insurrection was imminent. The I.R.B. and its members in the Irish Volunteers, however, were quietly preparing. The I.R.B. first organized a Military Committee in May 1915, later renamed the Military Council, to weld the I.R.B., the Irish Volunteers and Sinn Fein into a revolutionary instrument. Then, in early 1916, the two–hundred–strong Irish Citizen Army was brought into the coalition by James Connolly, its leader. He had remained aloof until this time because the revolutionaries had made no explicit commitment to a workers' republic. The I.R.B. had already decided in December 1915 that an insurrection should be planned for the following Easter, and Connolly now agreed to participate.

The decision to stage the Rising amazed John Devoy and the American Clan na Gael. Devoy wrote later: "They did not ask our advice; they simply announced a decision already taken; so, as we had already recognized the right of the Home Organization to make this supreme decision, our plain duty was to accept it and give them all the help we could."[7] Devoy did, indeed, give all the help he and the Clan na Gael could, and it was the fault of the revolutionaries in Ireland that the preparations for the Rising proved to be thoroughly confusing.

PREPARING FOR THE RISING

In February 1916, Devoy wrote to Berlin at the request of the I.R.B. requesting an arms shipment to land in Limerick on April 21 or 22, Good Friday or Easter Saturday. He asked that one hundred thousand rifles, artillery pieces, and German officers be sent. On March 4 the Germans offered twenty thousand rifles, ten machine guns, ammunition and explosives, but no officers. The shipment was scheduled to land in Tralee Bay between April 20 and 23. Devoy regarded this offer as inadequate but still believed that a rising could be staged. Using an alias to avoid detection, he

[7] Ward, p.105.

wrote to a friend about his new "position." "The salary is not as big as I expected, but it is a living wage and I am certain I would get a raise soon when they saw I could make good."[8] Casement, on the other hand, who was in Bavaria recovering from a mental and physical collapse, was completely disillusioned. He had already written on February 2, "So full of good–will, [the Germans] are swine and cads of the first order." He believed, correctly, that their offer was only made to impress the Irish in America and to create "some little complication for England in Ireland."[9] He decided to return to Ireland to stop the rising, and the Germans agreed to send him in a submarine. He left Germany on April 12, three days after the arms shipment.

A series of bizarre accidents now ensured that the entire German contribution would be wasted. A clumsy communications route between Ireland and Berlin—via the Clan na Gael and German diplomats in America, then via Berne or Amsterdam to Berlin—caused the final landing instructions from Ireland to arrive by wireless six days after the arms ship *Aud* had left Germany. The ship was travelling without a radio and could not be contacted. It arrived off Tralee on the night of April 20 knowing nothing of the new arrival time of nightfall on April 23 requested by the rebels. There was no one to receive the cargo. The ship waited in vain to be contacted for twelve hours and was arrested by the navy soon after setting out to sea. The *Aud* was then escorted to Queenstown, now known as Cobh, near Cork, where it was scuttled by its crew on April 22.

Casement himself arrived in Tralee Bay early on April 21, Good Friday, still with time to influence the Rising but several days later than he anticipated because of a mechanical breakdown that forced him to change submarines en route. He was captured, however, just a few hours after reaching the beach from his swamped landing craft. One of his two companions, Robert Monteith, who had been sent to Germany from Ireland to command

[8] Ward, p. 105.
[9] Ward, pp 101–102.

the Irish Brigade, escaped and made his way to the United States. But the second, Daniel Bailey, who was a member of the brigade, was captured and later collaborated with the British authorities. These events, the products of a cumbersome communications system and human error, were disastrous, of course, but events happening in Ireland were equally unfortunate. We have already noted the distinctive character of the Romantic Nationalism which Patrick Pearse shared with his I.R.B. colleagues, Thomas MacDonagh and Joseph Plunkett. The war presented them with an opportunity to make their blood sacrifice. In 1915, for example, Pearse insisted, "Ireland will not find Christ's peace until she has taken Christ's sword."[10] As Lyons explains, Pearse did not anticipate a military victory in a rising. Indeed, victory would come from not surviving. Pearse and his colleagues planned to sacrifice themselves for Ireland and, by their example, to inspire their countrymen.

Few of the revolutionaries shared Pearse's mystical vision. In the United States, Devoy and the Clan na Gael had always hoped that a rising would lead to a military victory. In Ireland, Tom Clarke and James Connolly believed in the power of example, but not necessarily the romantic notion of the blood sacrifice. Connolly, for example, believed that the war was an opportunity to destroy capitalism and was prepared to see the struggle begin in Ireland, though he would die in the process. Nonetheless, it was Pearse who set the tone of the Rising. For example, in a memorable eulogy at the grave of O'Donovan Rossa in 1915, he said, "Life springs from death; and from the graves of patriot men and women spring living nations. The Defenders of this Realm . . . think that they have pacified Ireland . . . but the fools, the fools, the fools—they have left us our Fenian dead, and while Ireland holds these graves, Ireland unfree shall never be at peace."[11]

The I.R.B. was forced to operate secretly within the Irish Volunteers because of a critical difference of opinion between the revolu-

[10] F. S. L. Lyons, *Ireland Since the Famine* (London, 1971), p. 336.
[11] Patrick Pearse, *The Best of Pearse*, edited by Proinsias MacAonghusa and Liam Ó Reágáin (Cork, 1967), p. 134.

tionaries and the Volunteer chief of staff, Eoin MacNeill. He favored the steady growth of Volunteer strength so that, at the war's end, Britain would face a resolute body of Nationalists in Ireland. He knew that a military success was simply out of the question, and he opposed the notion of the blood sacrifice. He knew that only a minority of the Volunteers were armed with rifles and that they were a very small minority in the country. MacNeill believed that they should only act during the war if the government was to attempt to systematically suppress the movement or if an attempt was made to apply military conscription in Ireland. If forced to act, MacNeill believed the Volunteers should resort to guerilla war and not risk a direct confrontation with the British army which they could only lose. He and Redmond had not separated in 1914 because of any fundamental disagreement over home rule, but rather because of Redmond's active support for the war. MacNeill believed that Ireland's first duty was to itself.

MacNeill sensed that he was not in complete control of the situation. In January 1916 he asked Connolly to restrain his revolutionary zeal because he feared it might provoke the government into suppressing all Nationalist activities. When rumors of an insurrection floated early in 1916, MacNeill sought an assurance from Pearse that there were no plans in hand. He continued to be suspicious, however, and in a memorandum in February, he argued that an insurrection should only be launched if there were a real chance of success and "not merely some future moral or political advantage which may be hoped for as the result of non–success."[12] He wrote: "I do not know at this moment whether the time and the circumstances will yet justify distinct revolutionary action, but of this I am certain, that the only possible basis for successful revolutionary action is deep and widespread popular discontent. We have only to look around us in the streets to realize

---

[12] F. X. Martin, "Eoin MacNeill and the Easter Rising," *Irish Historical Studies* 13: 47 (March 1961): 234.

that no such condition exists in Ireland."[13] On April 5 MacNeill insisted that no order other than routine should be issued from the Volunteer headquarters without his signature. But he could not restrain the plotters. The die had been cast.

The I.R.B. was determined on an insurrection at Easter and an elaborate plan was underway to deceive MacNeill. He had already agreed that the Volunteers should resist any attempt to suppress the organization. So when a document was published in the press on April 19 purporting to be an instruction from the Irish administration at Dublin Castle to arrest the Volunteer leaders, MacNeill agreed that preparations should be made to resist. In fact, the document was probably forged. Irish undersecretary Sir Matthew Nathan only asked for permission to arrest the leaders on Easter Sunday, April 23, after Casement and the *Aud* had been captured, and he had concluded that there was a German conspiracy.

On April 20, one of MacNeill's supporters, Bulmer Hobson, discovered that an order had gone out calling for a rising on April 23, and when challenged by MacNeill, Pearse finally revealed that an order had been issued. MacNeill was persuaded not to countermand it because of the confusion such an order would create in the Volunteers and because, he now learned for the first time, German arms supplies were en route. This was the first MacNeill knew of the German connection. By Saturday evening, April 22, however, he realized the full dimensions of the conspiracy. By then he knew that the *Aud* and Casement had been captured and that the Dublin Castle document was probably forged. Very early on Sunday morning—the planned date of the Rising—MacNeill issued a countermanding order which was immediately carried throughout Ireland, and in an advertisement placed in the *Sunday Independent* newspaper he prohibited all Volunteer maneuvers.

It would be unfair to blame MacNeill's order for the confusion outside Dublin and the general failure of the country to respond to the Rising when it did take place on Easter Monday. As Dangerfield makes clear, the rest of Ireland was woefully unprepared

[13] Martin, p. 240.

for a rebellion in the best of circumstances.[14] But MacNeill had made sure that there would be no Rising on Easter Sunday. Nevertheless, as Pearse had warned earlier, the countermanding order was not obeyed by all the Volunteers. Pearse and his associates were determined to continue the Rising and they rescheduled it for Easter Monday. As we saw in Chapter One, they led their forces out to certain military defeat at midday on April 24, believing that, in the words of the Proclamation of the Irish Republic, "Ireland, through us, summons her children to her flag and strikes for her freedom."

CONCLUSION

The Rising certainly took the British government by surprise. At one level this could be excused. It was clear in 1915 and 1916 that the Irish Volunteers, and seditious activities in general, were growing. But there was really no widespread disaffection, and the policy of the Irish administration—to contain the extremists but not to force them underground by a policy of suppression—was succeeding. There was, then, no reason to fear a general insurrection, and on April 10, Nathan, who had not been briefed by military intelligence, said that he did not believe one was planned. But a rising was being planned and the government, lulled by the relatively stable condition of Ireland, paid too little heed to the evidence.

In late March, the director of military intelligence informed General Friend, the commander in chief of Ireland, that wireless interceptions indicated that a rising was being planned for April 22 and that a request had been made for German assistance. The navy ordered strict patrolling of the Irish coast. On April 16, the naval authorities at Queenstown learned that an arms shipment and two submarines, both of which Casement used because his first broke down, had left Germany for Ireland. Augustine Birrell, the

[14] George Dangerfield, *The Damnable Question* (Boston, 1976), pp. 200-206.

chief secretary, Undersecretary Nathan, and Lord Lieutenant Wimborne were not told of these movements until April 17.

So there were certainly indications that something was being planned, but it is not true, as has been alleged, that the United States government alerted the British to the Rising and was responsible for Casement's capture. On April 18, 1916, American agents raided a New York advertising agency that was being used as a cover for German activities and thereby violating American neutrality. Papers were seized from German diplomat Wolf von Igel, for example, which revealed plans concerning Casement and the Rising. But none of this information was supplied to the British Embassy until after Casement and the *Aud* had been captured. In fact, Casement was captured by accident, and the *Aud* went undetected for a day. Even given these events and the warning from military and naval intelligence, the Irish adminstration saw no reason to fear an insurrection. They had enough information, it is true, by Easter Sunday to ask Birrell for permission to arrest the leaders of the Irish Volunteers for alleged complicity with the Germans. But they did not actually fear a rising and did not prepare for it. Indeed, the capture of Casement, whom they took to be a leader, the seizure of the *Aud*, and MacNeill's prohibition of maneuvers in the *Sunday Independent* confirmed the Irish adminstration's view that there was no longer any danger. General Friend was allowed to take his leave in England, and the army was relaxing when the Rising broke out on April 24, Easter Monday. What no one in the adminstration had appreciated was the very special mentality of the men who led their forces into the streets that day.

Part III. The Aftermath

8

Sinn Fein Emerges

Following the Fenian rising in 1867, an Irish magistrate, who understood that revolutions thrive on martyrs, cautioned the government with these words, "Let us not re–animate the feelings of Fenianism by making martyrs and exciting sympathy in their favor."[1] There were many convictions in 1867 but no executions and, consequently, no martyrs. In 1916, however, fifteen of the rebel leaders were executed within two weeks of the Rising, and by August the government had also executed Sir Roger Casement. Sixteen martyrs had been added to the Irish pantheon. Does this mean that Pearse and his colleagues had succeeded in their blood sacrifice? Had they, in Pearse's words, "saved Ireland's honour"? Did the Irish nation spring from the graves of these patriots, as Pearse had prophesied?

In an important sense, the answer to these questions is Yes. The Rising did inspire a revolution which culminated in Irish independence in 1922. But the answer is also No. It was not the Rising alone which produced this result but also the actions of the United Kingdom government. Wiser policies might have denied Pearse and his colleagues the victory for which they had died. The Rising was, after all, widely denounced in Ireland—although it must be admitted that the layer of Irish support for Britain was rather thin.

[1] Leon O Broin, *Fenian Fever: An Anglo–American Dilemma* (New York, 1971), p. 177.

As George Dangerfield observed, "Beneath that rather shallow feeling of agreement with the English cause as against the German, there lay for most Irishmen, to put it mildly, an inveterate and incurable distaste for English rule."[2] The United Kingdom government, therefore, had no easy task in trying to control the emotional aftermath of the Rising, but in these difficult circumstances it did very poorly.

TRIALS AND EXECUTIONS

The government's first mistake was to try the rebels by secret courts–martial and to execute the leaders. Tom Clarke was the first to die, by a firing squad in Kilmainham prison on May 3. By May 12, thirteen others had been executed in Dublin and one in Cork. Some of the executions were particularly poignant and made a deep impression when they become known. For example, James Connolly was seriously wounded during the Rising and had to be carried to his execution on a stretcher. Joseph Plunkett, who was already dying from tuberculosis, was married in his cell just hours before his execution. All seven of the signers of the Proclamation of Independence paid with their lives. Seventy–five death sentences were commuted but not before Irish opinion had been influenced by the executions.

The decision to execute the leaders was made in the heat of the moment, and it would have required enormous generosity for the government to forgive and forget a rebellion on such a scale and at such a time. Nevertheless, the executions were unwise because they aroused and focussed the latent hostility toward England—the sense of "we" and "they"—which had always existed in Ireland. John Redmond, who had condemned the Rising in the House of Commons on April 27, soon warned the government not to carry out the executions. John Dillon, his deputy who had witnessed the Rising firsthand in Dublin, insisted that they would destroy the standing of the Irish Party, the party of moderation

[2] George Dangerfield, *The Damnable Question* (Boston, 1976), p. 4.

and compromise, by making martyrs of the rebels. He savagely attacked the government in the House of Commons on May 11 after his advice had been rejected. "[You] are washing out our whole life work in a sea of blood," he cried, even expressing his pride in the rebels who had fought a clean fight.[3] The Catholic bishop of Limerick condemned the government for executing the leaders before any pleas for mercy could be made.

The government further damaged the standing of the Irish party in its fight for survival by putting Sir Roger Casement on trial for treason in London in June and by entrusting his prosecution to Sir F. E. Smith, the attorney general, who had been a leader of the Ulster rebels in the years before the war. Casement had actually returned to Ireland to stop the Rising, but he refused to plead the truth in his defense for fear of damaging the impact of the Rising. Instead, in a dramatic speech from the dock, he challenged the jurisdiction of the court and made a bold appeal for Ireland.

Casement placed the government in an embarrassing quandary. Asquith and his coalition colleagues, some of whom were staunch Unionists, believed that the rebels had to be punished for their treason. But it had become clear from police reports, for example, that Irish opinion was rapidly turning against the government. It had also become clear that American sentiment was generally with the rebels. Even sympathetic American newspapers, such as the New York *Times*, condemned the executions as incredibly stupid. The British ambassador, Sir Cecil Spring–Rice, wrote in May: "The great bulk of American public opinion, while it might excuse executions in hot blood, would very greatly regret an execution some time after the event. . . . It is far better to make Casement ridiculous than a martyr."[4] On July 29, the United States Senate, in the midst of a general campaign in America to save Casement,

---

[3] Cited in F. S. L. Lyons, "Dillon, Redmond, and the Irish Home Rulers," in F. X. Martin, *Leaders and Men of the Easter Rising: Dublin 1916* (Ithaca, N.Y. 1967), p. 35.
[4] Alan J. Ward, *Ireland and Anglo–American Relations, 1899–1921* (London, 1969), p. 114.

voted to urge the United Kingdom government to treat Irish political prisoners with clemency. The Cabinet knew that these hostile reactions in Ireland and America might impede the war effort, but with opinion in Britain to consider and an example to set, the decision to proceed with the execution on August 3 was made unanimously.

Casement had certainly not appreciated the symbolic importance of the Rising when he set out from Germany in April. He only knew that it was military madness which should be stopped. But by going back he unwittingly became a leading actor in the drama being directed by Pearse and he too became a martyr—the sixteenth—by his execution. His remains were belatedly transferred to a martyr's grave in Dublin in 1965.

ATTEMPTS TO CONCILIATE

The Easter Rising brought a new set of problems that the government could not ignore. With the exception of the death of Casement, all the executions were over by May 12, and it must be said that the story thereafter is not one of unrelieved repression. Both Prime Minister Asquith and his successor, David Lloyd George, made conciliatory gestures, but without success. Between May 12 and 19, Asquith was in Ireland investigating the Rising and on his return asked Lloyd George, then minister for munitions, to try once more to find a solution to the Irish problem. Asquith knew that Ireland was hampering the war effort at home, but he seemed to have been at least as concerned with the terrible impact of the Rising and executions on American opinion. Lloyd George shared his concern. "The Irish–American vote will go over to the German side," he argued. "The Americans will break our blockade and force an ignominious peace on us, unless something is done even provisionally to satisfy America."[5]

Lloyd George had been given a daunting assignment: to solve the insoluble Irish problem in the midst of a great war and follow-

[5] Ward, p. 113.

ing a treasonable rebellion. Neither of the protagonists of 1914 had changed their views. Indeed, the Rising had made them more intransigent than ever. To retain their credibility, the Irish Party had found it necessary to be more militantly separatist than ever while the Unionists were able to argue that the Rising proved conclusively the dangers to British security inherent in a self-governing Ireland. Lloyd George gave the appearance of some progress towards a solution but only by offering different terms to the two sides. John Redmond and the Irish Party believed that they were offered home rule subject only to the temporary exclusion of six Ulster counties. On the other hand, the Unionists believed they were offered permanent exclusion. When the proposals were introduced into the House of Commons late in July, they reflected the Unionist view and were immediately rejected by the Nationalists.

When Lloyd George himself became prime minister in a new coalition government on December 7, 1916, the Irish problem had several dimensions. First, a solution was important in itself. The problem had to be resolved. Second, so long as the government and the military were distracted by Ireland, they were also distracted from the war in Europe. Third, the Irish problem had an impact on relations with other countries. For example, two conscription referenda were defeated in Australia in 1916 and 1917 because of Irish–Australian opposition to the war. More important was the attitude of Irish Americans, both before and after America's entry into the war in April 1917. President Wilson himself appealed to Lloyd George to resolve the Irish question. When Arthur Balfour, Lloyd George's foreign secretary, was visiting the United States in May 1917, he reported: "The [Irish] question is apparently the only difficulty we have to face here, and its settlement would no doubt greatly facilitate the vigorous and lasting cooperation of the United States Government in the war."[6]

Lloyd George proved to be a brilliant war leader, but despite the enormous stakes involved, a solution for Ireland eluded him. At best he could give it only a small portion of his time. When it

[6] Ward, p. 149.

forced itself through the morass of war policy to the attention of the War Cabinet, he tended to view the problem not through his old eyes as a Welsh home ruler but through the eyes of the Unionist colleagues who dominated his coalition. His first major move was to accept John Redmond's suggestion that Irishmen of all parties and persuasions should be invited to a convention to try to settle the Irish problem among themselves. It was just possible that the Irish Convention which convened in July 1917 might arrive at a settlement, but the worst it could do was put the problem on ice for a while. Redmond died on March 6, 1918, just before the Convention completed its work.

Most of the people confined after the Rising had been released before the end of 1916; but the leaders still in prison—many of whom had originally been sentenced to death—were released before the Convention opened in an attempt to improve the climate of opinion in Ireland. The gesture proved to be futile when Sinn Fein, now recognized as the political arm of Revolutionary Nationalism, refused to participate in the meetings.

In April 1918 the Convention presented by a vote of 44 to 29 a report which advocated dominion government, that is, independence for a united Ireland under the crown, the status of Australia or Canada. Lloyd George deluded himself into believing that the report might provide the basis for a settlement, overlooking the fact that Sinn Fein had rejected the Convention and the Ulster Unionists had voted against the report because it did not provide for the exclusion of the North. No report could have been implemented without the consent of these two militant groups, and the fact that the Irish Party and the Southern Unionists, who had finally accepted the inevitability of Irish self–government, were in the majority had become almost irrelevant.

When faced with the breakdown of the convention, Lloyd George used British logic to blame the Irish as a whole for failing to agree and Unionist logic to blame the Nationalists in particular. "They are not satisfied with getting self–determination for themselves," he said, "without depriving others of the right of self-determination."[7]

THE COLLAPSE OF CONSTITUTIONAL NATIONALISM

Revolutionary Nationalism had not been crushed in the months of military rule which followed the Rising. There quickly developed, for example, what Lyons calls a "cult of the dead leaders," with frequent commemorative masses.[8] The survivors went underground and even those in prison began to organize to strike again on their release. By the end of 1916 those who had been imprisoned without trial were free, and those who had been convicted were released in June 1917.

The name Sinn Fein was now used everywhere to describe those who supported the goals of the Rising, and not simply the members of the organization founded by Arthur Griffith in 1907. But by March 1918, there were about 1,025 branches of Sinn Fein proper and 81,200 members. A sign of things to come occurred in January 1917 when Count George Plunkett, a Sinn Fein sympathizer and the father of Joseph Plunkett, ran as an independent in the North Roscommon by-election and defeated the Irish party candidate. He refused to take his seat in parliament.

There was no immediate and massive desertion to Sinn Fein, but the Irish Party could only survive if two conditions were met. First, it had to move into a posture of active opposition to the United Kingdom government. The old policy of moderation would not accommodate the new mood of Ireland. Second, the government could do nothing to encourage further unrest in Ireland because any worsening of the situation would benefit the extremists. Neither of these conditions was met and by the end of 1918, Constitutional Nationalism was a spent force.

John Redmond and his followers in the constitutional movement did attempt to satisfy the first condition. They condemned the

[7] Ward, p. 203.
[8] F. S. L. Lyons, *Ireland Since the Famine* (London, 1971) p. 381.

executions and rejected Lloyd George's proposals in 1916. By 1918, they had also dropped the policy of home rule, of limited autonomy for Ireland, and were demanding dominion status. But they never succeeded in building a new identity for the Irish Party. Indeed, policy was less important at this stage than posture, and the greater militancy of Sinn Fein was proving to be more attractive.

Sinn Fein won its first in a series of by–election victories when Plunkett was successful in North Roscommon in February 1917. In May, Joseph MacGuinness, who was still in prison, won South Longford with the endorsement of Dr. W. J. Walsh, the Archbishop of Dublin. In July, Eamon de Valera, newly released from prison and the senior surviving officer of the Rising, won East Clare. In August, William Cosgrave won the City of Kilkenny and in April 1918, Dr. Patrick McCartan won North King's County when the Irish Party failed to field a candidate. Finally, in June 1918 Arthur Griffith won in East Cavan. The Sinn Fein winners all refused to take their seats in the House of Commons. They were following the policy of withdrawal from Westminster outlined by Griffith many years before.

Meanwhile, in October 1917, Sinn Fein was reorganized as the official political arm of the republican movement, and de Valera was elected president of the party with its founder, Arthur Griffith, as vice president. De Valera was also elected president of the Irish Volunteers so that the political and military wings of the movement were united under a single leadership. The Irish Republican Brotherhood still existed but was no longer the force it had once been. De Valera, for one, refused to renew his membership in the organization.

Sinn Fein's progress did not mean that a tidal wave was engulfing the Irish Party. The party lost six seats to Sinn Fein but managed to win a number of by–elections, too. It won South County Dublin in July 1917; South Armagh, with the aid of Unionist votes, in February 1918; Waterford in March 1918, when Captain William Redmond—John Redmond's son—won his father's seat by a large margin; and East Tyrone in April 1918. But the party was in disarray. It failed to endorse the victorious constitutionalist candidate in West Cork in November 1916 for fear that he might lose, and when de Valera won East Clare, the London *Times* of July 12, 1917, reported, "Unfortunately the constitutional Nationalists are feeble and disunited." They failed altogether to enter a candidate in North King's County in April 1918 during the conscription crisis.

The second condition necessary for the survival of Constitutional Nationalism was that the government should not exacerbate the situation in Ireland after the executions. The fact that the military regime of General Maxwell continued until November 1916 did nothing to improve the atmosphere, and a midnight to 4:00 A.M. curfew was still in effect in Dublin until the end of July. Over eighteen hundred people were imprisoned without trial, and many were not released until December. These policies certainly antagonized a great number of people, but the real key to Ireland's state of mind lay in conscription.

Ireland had been excluded from conscription when it was introduced elsewhere in the United Kingdom in January 1916, because the government did not want to provoke Irish extremists. In the aftermath of the Rising, Ireland was even more sensitive, and in January 1917, the chief secretary, H. E. Duke, advised that unless Ireland was first offered home rule, Irish conscription would lead to "some bloodshed now and intensified animosities henceforward."[9] The prime minister appeared to agree, or so he told Redmond in December 1916.

On March 21, 1918, however, the Germans launched their greatest offensive of the war in France. The government believed that only a new batch of conscripts could solve the manpower shortage which had suddenly been exposed in France; and Ireland had the only large pool of untapped recruits in the United Kingdom—a number estimated at about one hundred sixty thousand.

[9] Alan J. Ward, Lloyd George and the 1918 Irish Conscription Crisis," *Historical Journal* 17: 1 (1974): 108–109.

On March 25, 1918, therefore, the War Cabinet made the decision to introduce a new bill to extend conscription in Britain and to introduce conscription to Ireland for the first time. Men were needed, and Ireland could not expect to be exempted from playing its full part in the war. This decision finally killed the Irish Party. As the English historian, D. C. Somervell, concluded, "Thus it was that the German offensive extinguished the last hopes of the typically Victorian compromise of Gladstonian Home Rule."[10]

The conscription decision went against almost all the advice the government had received from Ireland. For example, Chief Secretary Duke said on March 27, "We might almost as well recruit Germans."[11] The lord lieutenant, Lord Wimborne, head of the Royal Irish Constabulary; General Byrne, the Irish lord chief justice; Sir James Campbell, the Irish attorney general; James O'Connor; and even the Unionist leader, Sir Edward Carson, all advised that the value of the troops raised in Ireland would be outweighed by the cost of raising them.

The anticonscription protest from the Nationalists in Ireland was immediate, overwhelming, and unprecedented. It culminated in a remarkable meeting in the Mansion House, Dublin, on April 18, when John Dillon and Eamon de Valera led the Irish Party, Sinn Fein, the Irish Catholic bishops, and the Trades Unions in a pledge to resist conscription. A general strike was called for April 23. Nothing did more to legitimize Sinn Fein than its membership in this coalition which had been called into being by Irish conscription.

Until now, the government had accepted that conscription could not be implemented until home rule was in operation, and it was quickly forced back into this position by the adverse reaction to their conscription announcement in Ireland. In the last days of March, the War Cabinet agreed to link conscription to some unspecified measure of home rule. In the House of Commons, Lloyd

[10] D. C. Somervell, *The Reign of King George V: An English Chronicle* (New York, 1935) p. 271.
[11] Ward, "Lloyd George and Irish Conscription," p. 110.

George stated that this was necessary to satisfy public opinion in the Dominions and the United States, but his primary concern was actually the state of opinion in Ireland. He apparently believed that the report of the Irish Convention, which was due early in April, would provide the basis for an Irish settlement that would make conscription possible. The truth, however, is that home rule was no more possible in 1918 than it had been in 1914 or 1916. The two most important parties to the dispute, the Unionists and Sinn Fein, both rejected the Convention report.

When the Conscription Bill was introduced in the House of Commons on April 9, the government had to agree that its application in Ireland would be suspended to allow Parliament an opportunity to approve what Lloyd George termed "a measure of self-government for Ireland."[12] The bill was approved in this form on April 16 and received the royal assent two days later. But the damage had been done. The government had finally committed itself to Irish conscription that could be implemented at any time by an Order in Council—that is, by an order of the government without reference to Parliament. John Dillon led the Irish Party out of the House of Commons, protesting that Ireland would not be seduced by a vague promise of self-government.

In the few weeks it had taken to put conscription on the statute books, disorder had grown in Ireland and the government had committed more mistakes. On April 11, for example, Lloyd George entrusted his Irish policy to a Cabinet committee chaired by Walter Long, a Tory who had been the leader of the Ulster Unionists from 1906 to 1911. His sympathies lay almost entirely with Ulster, but he had recently become a federalist. His preference for an Irish settlement within the framework of a federal scheme for the whole United Kingdom required radical constitutional surgery and could certainly not be implemented in time to save conscription. In any case, Long's efforts would have been ruined by the War Cabinet's decision of April 16 to send a general, Lord French, to Ireland to conduct an investigation. French re-

12 Ward, p. 114.

ported back that order could be restored and conscription secured by the application of force. The Irish, he insisted, had simply been misled by a minority of radicals! He was completely wrong. But early in May, French, an insensitive man with poor judgement who had already failed as commander of the British forces in France, was appointed to succeed Wimborne as lord lieutenant, and Edward Shortt replaced H. E. Duke as chief secretary. Lloyd George had acted on the dictum that if you don't like the advice, change the advisor. His reward was that the situation steadily worsened.

French, the "military governor," as Wimborne called him,[13] extended martial law to most of the Nationalist portions of the country and banned a host of meetings, newspapers and organizations—including Sinn Fein and the Gaelic League—but he could do nothing to prevent the situation from deteriorating. Most of Sinn Fein's leaders were arrested on May 17 and 18 and imprisoned without trial after the government claimed to have discovered a German plot in Ireland. The evidence, most of which related to the period of the Easter Rising two years earlier, could not have secured convictions in a court of law. In these circumstances, of course, home rule was impossible and so too was conscription. Nonetheless, the government insisted on standing by both policies, and it was still discussing them when the war ended in November 1918.

No general elections had been held in the United Kingdom since December 1910, and as soon as the war ended, Lloyd George dissolved Parliament and went to the people. The elections which were held on December 14, 1918, finally destroyed the Irish Party and Constitutional Nationalism. Sinn Fein contested all but two Irish constituencies, with forty–seven of their candidates still in prison. The Irish Party contested only fifty–nine constituencies in Ireland and one in England, the Liverpool seat of the veteran home ruler, T. P. O'Connor. They were not completely dismissed at the polls, as the table makes clear. They drew a large number

[13] Ward, p. 117.

General Election of 14 December 1918					
Party	Total Votes	M.P.'s Elected	Candidates Entered	Unopposed	Percent of Total U.K. Vote
Unionist	292,722	25	38	—	2.7
Irish Party	238,477	7°	60	1	2.2
Sinn Fein	486,867	73	102	25	4.5
°Including one seat in Liverpool					

Source: David Butler and Jennie Freeman, *British Political Facts*, 1900-1960 (London, 1963), p. 122.

of votes and they and the Unionists were able to deny Sinn Fein a majority of the total vote in Ireland. The truly devastating figure, however, was the number of seats won by each party. The Unionists did well in Protestant–dominated constituencies with twenty-five seats, but the Irish Party won only six seats in Ireland as opposed to seventy–three won by Sinn Fein. Even John Dillon, the leader of the party, was defeated by Eamon de Valera in Mayo. The Irish Party had been routed and it quickly disappeared from view. But we cannot say that the electors were voting for either a republic or a revolution. They had always supported constitutionalists before, and they would again in 1922, but for the moment they had lost their belief in the party of moderation and had nowhere to turn but to Sinn Fein, the party led by the rebels of 1916.

CONCLUSION

Although the government had made many mistakes since the Easter Rising, few compare with those in the disastrous year of 1918. Caution should have dictated that the Irish question be left alone, but Lloyd George and the War Cabinet overruled the overwhelming majority of experts in Ireland and decided on conscription. To formulate a new home rule plan, the prime minister nominated Walter Long. To quell the growing disorder, the Cabinet sent Lord French to impose military rule. To suppress Sinn Fein, they arrested the leaders on the unsupported pretext that there existed a German plot. The result was the rapid expansion of Sinn Fein caused not by a wholesale conversion to Revolutionary Nationalism and the principles of the Easter Rising but by a popular reaction to the government's behavior. The great irony is that the army managed to survive in France without Irish conscripts.

9
A Victory for
Revolutionary Nationalism

DAIL EIREANN

Sinn Fein did not win a majority of the Irish vote in 1918, but it accepted the election result as a mandate for the establishment of a parliament for the Irish Republic which had been proclaimed by Pearse at the G.P.O. in 1916. The party had campaigned on a platform which included (1) Ireland's withdrawal from Westminister, (2) the establishment of an Irish assembly in Dublin and (3) an appeal to the peace conference about to assemble in Paris for recognition of the Irish Republic. This program was immediately implemented. Sinn Feiners refused to take their seats in the House of Commons, and instead twenty–seven of those who were not in prison attended the first session of Dail Eireann, the Irish Parliament, at the Mansion House in Dublin on January 21, 1919. One of their first acts was to appoint three delegates to the peace conference: de Valera and Griffith, who were still in prison, and Count Plunkett.

On January 22, Dail Eireann established a government for Ireland with Cathal Brugha at its head and four other members, Eoin MacNeill, Michael Collins, Count Plunkett and Richard Mulcahy. By March, those Sinn Feiners arrested in the "German plot" of 1918 had been released or, as in the case of de Valera, had already escaped, and fifty–two members were able to attend Dail Eireann on April 1 when de Valera was elected to succeed Brugha as Priomh–Aire, or first minister, of the Irish government. Dail Eireann could not expect to be a fully effective legislature. It was banned by the United Kingdom government in September 1919 and went underground. It met only six times in 1919, three times in 1920 and four times in 1921. Sinn Fein's sweeping victories in local government elections in January and May of 1920, however, gave the republicans control of local administration in most of Catholic Ireland. The Dail was able to introduce a court system in 1919 which effectively replaced the United Kingdom system in much of the country by the following year.

THE WAR OF INDEPENDENCE

As Sinn Fein made these advances in the political and judicial spheres, the military wing of the republican movement was beginning the guerilla war which brought independence in 1922. The guerillas came to be known as the Irish Republican Army, but command was complicated by the continued underground existence of both the I.R.B. and the Irish Volunteers. Dail Eireann was never in complete control of the military situation before the truce in 1921. The pace of the war was set by the I.R.B. operating within the Volunteers. Cathal Brugha was de Valera's minister of defense, but Michael Collins, the minister for finance, came to control the war as president of the I.R.B.

By August 1919, the war was seriously under way, and in the following two years, Collins pioneered twentieth–century guerrilla war. He was a survivor of the battle at the G.P.O. in 1916, but no military strategy could have been further removed from that experience than the war of independence. There was, Charles Townshend observed, a new realism in stark contrast to the blood sacrifice of 1916.[1] The Easter Rising was a siege campaign fought

---

[1] Charles Townshend, *The British Campaign in Ireland, 1919–1921* (London, 1975), p. 66.

from fixed positions in the center of Dublin but now Collins and his men, who were poorly armed until they had captured enough equipment from the government in 1919, moved in small, highly mobile units that attacked at points of weakness, generally in Dublin and the south and west of Ireland. They employed tactics of ambush, terror, intimidation and selective brutality against the police primarily, but also against Irish collaborators and the army. If challenged, they withdrew into sanctuaries—the countryside, mountains, or areas with sympathetic populations. J. Boywer Bell, a specialist on guerilla wars, writes that Ireland was not particularly good country for guerillas.[2] It lacked good roads, its terrain was too open and its wild areas lacked food supplies. It could support only a limited number of guerillas and, indeed, the I.R.A. numbered only about five thousand hard–core fighters. But their greatest asset was the sanctuary offered by a sympathetic population. The army and police suffered from extremely poor intelligence information throughout the war because, as Townshend writes, "Their 'intelligence gap' resulted from [the republicans'] overwhelming psychological domination of the community. The rebels of 1920 were the heirs not only to the exalted legacies of the United Irishmen and the Fenians, but also to a deeper and darker tradition of agrarian secret society terrorism."[3] The majority of Irish Catholics may have been neither proterror nor prorepublic but they would not betray the I.R.A.

The United Kingdom government fought a disorganized and unsophisticated campaign. The military and police were never properly integrated, and both used poorly trained men. They could only hope to defeat the republicans with overwhelming power because the task of defending all possible targets against attack and searching out the hidden attackers could only be accomplished by large forces. The army had about forty thousand men and the police, with auxiliaries, about seventeen thousand;

[2] J. Bowyer Bell, *The Secret Army: A History of the I.R.A.* (Cambridge, Massachusetts, 1970), p. 23.
[3] Townshend, pp. 63–64.

but the army commander, General Macready, wanted a total of one hundred thousand. Even with overwhelming numbers, however, guerillas are almost impossible to defeat if they operate within a sympathetic population. The republicans did not anticipate a military victory. Instead, they were primarily concerned with propaganda. Their objectives were to prove that the United Kingdom could not govern Ireland peacefully and to convince it to withdraw. The government's military response played into the republicans' hands by transforming Ireland into a harsh military regime. This alienated still further the Nationalist parts of the country. There were no large fixed battles, but for a country with a small population the casualties were substantial. Lyons estimates that in 1920, 230 soldiers and police were killed and 369 wounded. In the whole period from January 1919 until July 1921, the I.R.A. suffered 752 dead and 866 wounded.[4]

It was a war filled with dramatic incidents which fuelled the folklore of Irish patriotism. In March 1920, for example, the lord mayor of Cork, Thomas MacCurtain, was murdered in his home, probably by police. His successor, Terence MacSwiney, died in prison the following October 25 after a long and highly publicized hunger strike. A week later the British executed Kevin Barry, an eighteen–year–old student, for his role in an ambush that killed six soldiers. In March 1920 the hated Black and Tans, a group of approximately twelve hundred auxiliary police, began to operate in Ireland. They were recruited in Britain because of the understandable shortage of new recuits in Ireland. Because of a supply shortage, they wore the khaki tunics of the army and dark green hats and trousers of the police, hence their customary name. They were a brutal and undisciplined group who lashed out ferociously at the I.R.A. in what Townshend describes as "police counter-terrorism."[5] Indeed, most of the atrocities committed by government forces were attributable to these and other police auxiliaries

[4] F. S. L. Lyons, *Ireland Since the Famine* (London, 1971), p. 415.
[5] Townshend, p. 113.

in 1920. On November 21, for example, after twelve British intelligence officers had been brutally murdered by the I.R.A. in Dublin, the police turned a routine search operation of a sports crowd at Croke Park, Dublin, into a shooting spree which killed twelve people.

The army was better disciplined but was not immune to charges of terror and intimidation. For example, it engaged in approximately one hundred fifty "official" reprisals from December 1920 until the truce in July 1921 which destroyed a large number of cooperative creameries and other buildings. These acts may have been provoked by the I.R.A., but one of the purposes of a guerilla campaign is to use calculated provocation to force the government into participating in the breakdown of law and order. The government then becomes the greater enemy. Irish Nationalists have always condemned the government's brutality during the war, but the brutality was a sure sign that the I.R.A. campaign was succeeding.

The government could think of no policy but coercion in Ireland. Townshend argues: "By and large the Cabinet adhered to the "murder gang" theory—the belief that the majority of the Irish people were not hostile but were terrorized by a small group of fanatics—and based on it a dual policy of 'crushing murder' while reconciling the 'moderates.' But no real attempt was made to assess the strength and outlook, or even to prove the existence, of this moderate group on which the whole policy hinged."[6] The most conspicuous act of coercion was the Restoration of Order Act of August 1920 which suspended habeas corpus and granted considerable powers and immunities to the military, including secret courts–martial. Prior to this act, there had been not one conviction for murder in a crown court since the shooting began in 1919.

[6] Townshend, p. 203

DE VALERA IN AMERICA

In June 1919, soon after he became the leader of the Irish government, Eamon de Valera left secretly for the United States where for the next eighteen months, as the war developed in Ireland, he campaigned for an Irish republic.[7] Indeed, he was introduced at gatherings throughout the country as the president of the Irish Republic.

The Irish–American opposition to Britain had largely been suspended during the period of America's participation in the war in 1917 and 1918, but it reemerged in 1919. Politicians throughout the United States, fed a somewhat exaggerated diet of British atrocities and Irish sufferings, jumped on the Irish Nationalist bandwagon. The movement was still led by Daniel Cohalan and John Devoy, veterans of the Clan na Gael and prewar Revolutionary Nationalism, and their new vehicle was an organization founded in March 1916, the Friends of Irish Freedom, which grew to approximately two hundred seventy five thousand members in 1919.

De Valera and Cohalan soon developed a mutual antipathy. Their temperaments clashed and so did their principles. They represented very different interests. Cohalan had always seen the Irish problem through American eyes and believed British imperialism was as great a threat to America as to Ireland. He insisted that Irish Americans should work to oppose British foreign–policy interests in general and Anglo–American cooperation in particular. De Valera, on the other hand, was interested only in Ireland and had no quarrel with Anglo–American harmony. He wanted Irish Americans to fight *for* Ireland, not *against* Britain.

Cohalan and John Redmond had already fought over this issue between 1900 and 1914, in addition to their differences over Revo-

---

[7] De Valera's visit to America is described in Alan J. Ward, *Ireland and Anglo–American Relations, 1899–1921* (London, 1969), chap. 10.

lutionary Nationalism. Redmond had managed to weaken Cohalan's influence by organizing the United Irish League of America, which took control of the Irish–American mass movement. De Valera did not disagree with Cohalan over the merits of revolutionary action, but he too challenged Cohalan's leadership of the Irish Americans and his perception of Ireland's role in Anglo–American relations. This was an issue of great importance to Cohalan because he was at least as determined to defeat President Wilson's peace program and the League of Nations—which he regarded as a British plot—as he was to win Irish independence. De Valera was extremely angry that the Irish Victory Fund—a large sum of money raised by the Friends of Irish Freedom—was being used primarily in the campaign to defeat the League.

Cohalan certainly had some successes. He did much to publicize Ireland's cause. He organized a great Irish Race Convention in Philadelphia in March 1919, that sent three Americans to lobby the peace conference in Paris. He mobilized a campaign which led the House of Representatives to approve, by a vote of 216 to 45 on March 4, a resolution asking the peace conference to favorably consider the claims of Ireland to the right of self–determination. The same campaign led the United States Senate to approve, by a vote of 60 to 1 on June 6, a resolution asking the American peace commission to secure a hearing for the representatives of Dail Eireann. The peace conference never did recognize Ireland, or even discuss the issue officially, but these activities dramatized the Irish cause. Cohalan had a more direct impact on American foreign policy, however, because the Irish Americans were an immensely powerful element in the coalition which managed to defeat the League of Nations in the Senate. In March 1920, they were rewarded when the Senate added a fifteenth reservation to the fourteen which had already caused Wilson to abandon the League. It called for Irish self–determination.

De Valera never succeeded in taking control of the Friends of Irish Freedom or curbing Cohalan's activities. On the other hand, Cohalan recognized de Valera's standing in the eyes of Irish Americans and could do nothing to destroy his image or effectiveness. Indeed, each drew support from essentially the same pool of Irish Americans. De Valera's visit to the United States therefore proved to be very successful. He knew that he could never win official American recognition for the Irish Republic, but he was received very seriously by the press and the public as the representative of the Irish people, and he was a magnificent publicist for Ireland. The new organization which he founded, the American Association for the Recognition of the Irish Republic, was not a great success; but he was able to reestablish the United States as the major source of funding for Irish nationalism it had been before World War I. Five and a half million dollars worth of certificates were sold which could be redeemed for official government bonds as soon as Irish independence was internationally recognized. Furthermore, as leader, de Valera was able to restablish the unity of the Irish in Ireland and America which Redmond had lost when World War I broke out in 1914.

There was, of course, one great difference between 1914 and 1920. Redmond was a constitutionalist but de Valera was a revolutionary and a survivor of the Easter Rising. This does not mean, however, that Irish Americans flocked to de Valera because they had been radicalized by the Easter Rising and its aftermath. It means, rather, that they were always willing to support a leader the Irish themselves had chosen, be it Parnell, Redmond, or de Valera. Irish Americans were relatively unaware of the differences between home rule and republican independence, but they had always believed that the Irish at home should be supported in their demand for self–government. In the context of 1919, this meant endorsing Sinn Fein and Revolutionary Nationalism.

De Valera left the United States in December 1920, but the incredible agitation which he and Cohalan had promoted carried on. The Friends of Irish Freedom and the American Association for the Recognition of the Irish Republic both continued their work. The Committee of One Hundred on Conditions in Ireland—a group of governors, senators, congressmen, mayors and religious leaders—was organized and published a report in March 1921 which drew a desperate and exaggerated view of the effects of the war in Ireland. The American Committee for Relief in Ireland was founded, with an equally eminent list of patrons, and it, too, presented an exaggerated view of the distress and destruction caused by the war. It raised five and a quarter million dollars for relief in Ireland, a sum which went to Sinn Fein.

It was clear from all of these activities that unless a settlement could be reached the war in Ireland was going to be fuelled indefinitely by American money, and Anglo-American relations would never improve.

THE GOVERNMENT OF IRELAND ACT, 1920

De Valera had been in Ireland for six months when Lloyd George introduced a new plan for Ireland. In November 1919 a Cabinet committee chaired by Walter Long had reported: "The Committee are agreed that in view of the situation in Ireland itself, of public opinion in Great Britain, and still more of public opinion in the Dominions and the United States of America, they cannot recommend the policy either of repealing or postponing the Home Rule Act of 1914."[8] The act would have to be amended. The committee proposed that two home rule parliaments be established in Ireland, and this proposal was presented to Parliament as the Government of Ireland Bill in December. It became law a year later in December 1920. Twenty-six counties were to be included in a Southern Ireland Parliament in Dublin. Six counties, including two with Nationalist majorities—Fermanagh and Tyrone—were to be included in a Northern Ireland Parliament in Belfast. There is no evidence that the Unionists wanted home rule for themselves. They would still have preferred simple exclusion from home rule and the continuation of government from Westminster, the solution which they had supported in 1914. But foreign policy considerations largely dictated that self-determination should be granted

[8] Ward, p. 227.

to the whole of Ireland, albeit in two parts. Lord Hugh Cecil was correct when he attacked the bill in the House of Lords and insisted, "We are here face to face with an attempt to satisfy foreign opinion, American opinion, opinion of the Dominions; we are not faced with any real attempt to govern Ireland."[9]

The new home rule proposals were very similar to those of 1886, 1893, and 1912. The important exceptions were that they would apply to two Parliaments, not one; and a Council of Ireland, composed of representatives from both Parliaments, would coordinate certain all–Ireland activities and plan for the eventual unification of the country. The two parliaments would control most of their domestic affairs, but the United Kingdom would retain control of ninety percent of Ireland's tax revenues, and the supremacy of the Westminster Parliament was explicitly affirmed in the act. Neither part of Ireland would be independent. There was no possibility of Sinn Fein accepting such a limited measure of self–government because it insisted that an Irish Republic had been in existence since 1916. But the Ulster Unionists did accept the act because it guaranteed that they would never be absorbed into the Dublin Parliament without their consent.

Elections for the two Parliaments were held in May 1921, with predictable results. Unionists won forty of the fifty–two seats in the Northern Parliament, which was opened by King George V on June 22, 1921. Sinn Fein was unopposed in all but four of the seats for the Southern Parliament—the seats of the Protestant Dublin University—but it actually used the elections as an inexpensive way of selecting a larger Dail Eireann. Sinn Fein members boycotted the first session of the southern Parliament on June 28, and it was immediately suspended. Southern Ireland became a crown colony.

[9] Ward, p. 226.

THE SETTLEMENT

De Valera returned to Ireland in December 1920 as the Government of Ireland act was being passed and at a time when the United Kingdom government believed Sinn Fein was losing ground. The government welcomed his return and took pains not to arrest him, believing he was a moderate who might accept a compromise settlement, not an extremist like Michael Collins. But the war did not decline in 1921. The number of I.R.A. operations actually grew from three hundred a week in April to five hundred a week in May, and one fourth of all the British casualties in the war since January 1919 were suffered between May 1921 and the truce on July 11.

The war did not abate, but de Valera was open to negotiations. In May 1921, he met with Sir James Craig, who was soon to become the first prime minister of Northern Ireland, but it was not until the Northern Parliament had been opened on June 22 that Lloyd George made an offer of negotiations which de Valera could accept. For the first time, there was no requirement that Sinn Fein surrender before talks could begin. Now that Northern Ireland was permanently protected by its own Parliament, Lloyd George could begin to deal seriously with Sinn Fein. Furthermore, the war had reached a stalemate. The government could win, but only by raising the conflict to a much higher level by more than doubling the number of troops in Ireland. De Valera accepted the offer of negotiations, and a truce was agreed for July 11. He and Lloyd George began their talks in London on July 14, 1921.

Lloyd George was prepared to offer the twenty–six counties of the South dominion status under the crown, that is, the status already enjoyed by Canada, Australia, New Zealand and South Africa. This amounted to an offer of virtual independence, although the constitutional status of the dominions was then in transition and was not fully clarified until 1931. Furthermore, the government insisted on retaining access to certain naval facilities in the South. This offer required the Irish Nationalists to sacrifice two critically important goals of the Easter Rising, a united Ireland and an Irish Republic. Northern Ireland would remain a separate entity with its own parliament, and the South would have to accept the king, as had the other dominions. De Valera refused these terms and would only concede that Ireland would sign a treaty of association with the British Commonwealth. He would recognize the crown as head of the Commonwealth, not as head of the Irish state, and he would swear no oath of allegiance to the crown.

De Valera chose not to travel to London in October for the final negotiations. Instead, he sent Arthur Griffith, Michael Collins, George Gavan Duffy, Robert Barton and E. J. Duggan, with Erskine Childers as secretary. On December 6, after long and terribly difficult negotiations, and under extreme pressure, they signed a treaty which accepted the essentials of Lloyd George's offer to de Valera. There would be an independent, twenty–six–county Ireland with dominion status under the crown, and the United Kingdom would retain naval facilities in the new state. The only significant concession by Lloyd George was a boundary commission to review the line of the Northern Ireland border.

The Irish delegates had been assured by Lloyd George that their refusal to sign would lead to a full–scale war in Ireland which would destroy republicanism. They yielded and a settlement was reached, but it was not the settlement which would bring peace to Ireland. Indeed, a great tragedy was in the making. The republicans were about to fight each other in a civil war over the terms of the treaty. Ironically, Michael Collins, the military commander considered an extremist by the United Kingdom government, accepted the settlement and de Valera, the moderate, rejected it.

Griffith and his colleagues on the negotiating team believed that they had legal authority to sign the treaty in London on behalf of the Dail Eireann government, but de Valera insisted that they should first have sought the approval of the ministers remaining in Dublin. When the document was considered by the full government, it won approval by only four votes to three with de Valera and two uncompromising republicans, Cathal Brugha and Austin Stack, insisting that Ireland should fight on for a united republic. In the majority were Arthur Griffith, Michael Collins, William Cosgrave, and Robert Barton. Their view, argued most strongly by Griffith and Collins, was that Lloyd George and his colleagues simply would not concede either a united Ireland or a republic. The I.R.A. had forced them to negotiate but could not win a military victory, and the treaty was the best that could be secured under the circumstances. It recognized Ireland's right to self-government and legal equality within the Commonwealth and provided the basis for the full freedom that would ultimately come. It was "not the ultimate freedom that all nations aspire and develop to, but the freedom to achieve it," Collins insisted.[10] It was widely believed by the protreaty majority that the boundary commission would so limit the size of Northern Ireland that it would soon choose to join the South.

The close division within the government was reflected in Dail Eireann where the treaty was only approved on January 7, 1922, by a vote of sixty–four to fifty–seven. De Valera then left the Dail temporarily with his supporters, and Arthur Griffith was elected head of the Irish government. The United Kingdom still refused to recognize Dail Eireann or Griffith's role. Instead, it acknowledged Michael Collins as head of a provisional administration nominated by the Southern Ireland home rule Parliament, which was technically reconvened for this purpose. But Collins and Griffith prepared together for the difficult transition to the new Irish Free State. The process was a stormy one.

Collins and Griffith tried desperately for a compromise with de Valera, but without success because they could secure his cooperation only by violating the treaty and alienating the British. The general election of June 24, 1922, for the new Dail Eireann of the Irish Free State was therefore fought on the issue of the treaty. The protreaty forces won fifty–eight seats with 620,283 votes. The

[10] Lyons, p. 442.

antitreaty forces won only thirty–five seats with 133,864 votes. The remaining 247,226 votes were shared between Labour, with seventeen seats, independents and farmers with seven each, and Dublin University, with four seats. When the minor parties and independents were included, the protreaty forces had won a clear majority of seats and an overwhelming majority in the popular vote.

THE CIVIL WAR

De Valera's republicanism had been defeated in the treaty negotiations, in Dail Eireann, and now at the polls, but the first shots had already been heard in the civil war. He had predicted war if his demands were not met, but he was not really in control of the republican extremists. Instead he found himself following in their wake. In a partial replay of the Easter Rising, an antitreaty group had occupied the Four Courts in Dublin in April. Collins' decision to dislodge them on June 28 marked the first major confrontation of the war.

The civil war took the form of sporadic guerilla attacks and reprisals. It was fought, initially, between the protreaty and antitreaty factions of the I.R.A. but the protreaty forces were soon formally organized as the army of the new state and grew to about thirty–five thousand men. The antitreaty republicans numbered about eight thousand when they were forced to surrender on May 24, 1923. By then approximately five hundred people had died and about thirteen thousand republicans were prisoners. Seventy-seven republicans had been executed in less than a year, compared with twenty–four executions carried out by the British in 1920 and 1921. It had been a savage war, but not, it now appears, an unusual one. Desmond Williams has observed that civil wars commonly follow revolutions conducted in the name of liberty—in France and the Soviet Union, for example. Such wars share a common pattern. Williams writes: "The old order is gone; the new one waits to be shaped . . . in such wars the parties and persons involved think they have a monopoly of righteousness. Human life has less value, for those engaged grow used to giving and taking death as the fever proceeds."[11]

CONCLUSION

Ireland paid a heavy price for the civil war. There were, of course, the dead and the wounded and the normal material losses of any armed conflict; but there were also deep psychological wounds. This was a war between enemies who had recently been friends and, as Williams writes, "When friends fall out, the daggers stay sharp."[12] Their quarrel was over the most fundamental revolutionary principle, the fulfillment of the republic which Pearse had declared at the G.P.O. in 1916. Collins and Griffith could argue that a settlement was militarily necessary and politically prudent, but de Valera could take the high ground by accusing them of betraying the republican ideal. Pearse and Connolly and the rest had not died so that Ireland could have dominion status and an oath of allegiance to the king. De Valera said during the treaty debate, "I am against the Treaty because it does not do the fundamental thing."[13] Ireland was a historic nation, not a British settlers' dominion.

The issue of the betrayal of the republic was the central issue in the debate on the treaty in the Dail. The failure to secure a united Ireland was an important but secondary concern. Dangerfield has recently argued that, if the Irish delegation had refused to sign the treaty in London and had remained faithful to the republic, "It is as certain as anything can be that there would have been no war."[14] He believed that the British were bluffing when they threatened to resume the war of independence. By this

[11] Desmond Williams, ed., *The Irish Struggle, 1916–1926* (London, 1966), p. 117.
[12] Williams, p. 118.
[13] Cited by Nicholas Mansergh, "Ireland and the British Commonwealth of Nations: the Dominion Settlement," in Williams, p. 138.
[14] George Dangerfield, *The Damnable Question* (Boston, 1976), p. 345.

interpretation, the Irish negotiators in London—Griffith, Collins, Duffy, Barton and Duggan—become responsible for the civil war because they did not have to sign the treaty. Had they not signed, there would have been no need for de Valera and his supporters to reject the treaty and there would have been no civil war.

Whether the British were or were not bluffing is still in doubt for many historians, but even if Dangerfield's assumption is correct and the British would not have resumed the war, his conclusion can be challenged. Consider the following sequence of events. First, Collins and Griffith believed that the British would resume the war, which the Irish would lose, if the delegation refused to sign the treaty. Second, the Irish delegation did sign the treaty. Third, it was accepted by a majority of the Irish republican government. Fourth, it was accepted by a majority of Dail Eireann. The decision to accept the treaty had already been made, therefore, for good or ill and by the elected representatives of Ireland, when the antitreaty faction decided to continue the war. Furthermore, the protreaty position was supported by the voters. By this interpretation the antitreaty faction must be held responsible.

Given that the treaty had already been signed and legally accepted before the civil war started, our evaluation of the behavior of the antitreaty faction has to hinge on whether the treaty represented a worthwhile settlement, and not on whether the British were bluffing. It was not a perfect treaty, but was it worth having? The majority of the people of Southern Ireland appeared to think so but revolutions are never democratic and patriots do not wait for a referendum before they act. The people of Ireland had not been consulted in 1916 and the antitreaty republicans did not consult them in 1922. As Dangerfield astutely observed, "A revolutionary minority . . . consults only what it believes the will of the people ought to be."[15]

The treaty provided the twenty–six county Irish Free State with legal equality with the United Kingdom and other members of the British Commonwealth. It was also offered full independence in

[15] Dangerfield, p. 345.

its domestic affairs and an opportunity for a new boundary settlement. There were ambiguities and uncertainties in the treaty, but in the following years all but one of these, the boundary issue, were resolved in favor of the new Irish state. The Statute of Westminster of 1931 reinforced Irish independence by clarifying dominion status. The oath of allegiance was dropped by Dail Eireann in 1932, and there was nothing the United Kingdom could do to prevent this. Other changes in Ireland's relations with the crown followed before the completely new constitution was adopted in 1937 and the Irish Free State became Eire. In 1938, negotiations with the United Kingdom led to it abandoning its naval rights in Southern Ireland. Finally, in 1949 Eire formally became the Republic of Ireland and withdrew from the British Commonwealth. In the same year, India became a republic and remained *within* the Commonwealth. It continued to recognize the crown only as head of the Commonweath. When de Valera had offered this as "external association" in 1921, he had been rebuffed by Lloyd George. His rejection of the treaty and the civil war had followed. Now the Irish Republic had no interest in the concept. To use Desmond Williams' phrase, "By the time the British found the answer, the Irish had lost interest in the question."[16] Ireland and the United Kingdom remained very closely associated but the Irish Republic was fully independent, with none of the legal ties of old to bind it, no matter how loosely. It was ironic that this final step was taken by a coalition government led by Fine Gael, the party which had evolved from the protreaty faction of 1922.

The one great setback for the South after 1922 was that the boundary commission, made up of a Unionist, a South African judge, and Eoin MacNeill (who represented the Free State), ruled in 1925 that there should be no alteration in the border with Northern Ireland. MacNeill dissented, but the Free State was forced to accept the existing partition with the North.

There were, then, both good and bad effects flowing from the treaty, and the antitreaty faction might reasonably argue that the

[16] Williams, p. 139.

bad—the failure of the boundary commission—justified the civil war. But this argument lost its force in 1926 when de Valera, who had been released from prison in 1924, formed a new democratic party, Fianna Fail. He left behind a small minority in Sinn Fein and the I.R.A. who were never to give up the struggle for a republic but he, too, betrayed the republican ideal. In 1927, Fianna Fail contested the general election, won forty–four seats, and took those seats as the second largest party in Dail Eireann. In 1932, it won seventy seats, enough to form the government, and de Valera became prime minister of the Irish Free State, the regime he had fought only ten years before. It was his government which peacefully removed the oath of allegiance and reformed the constitution; but it was also his government which banned the I.R.A. in 1936 and suspended normal legal processes to suppress the organization during its campaign of dynamite sabotage in Britain in 1939. By the end of World War II, the governments of Eire, Northern Ireland, and the United Kingdom had combined to virtually destroy the I.R.A. The knowledge that de Valera and most of his antitreaty supporters had accepted the Irish Free State in 1927—though under protest—had come to govern it in 1932 and had used the powers of the state to suppress the remnants of the antitreaty republicans makes it extremely difficult to condone their behavior in 1922. The civil war was unnecessary.

The civil war had a profound effect on Irish political life. For example, Fine Gael and Fianna Fail, the two major parties in contemporary Ireland, are the descendants of the pro and antitreaty factions respectively. Both have changed with the times, but the relatively nonideological character of Irish politics is due largely to the fact that the fundamental cleavage in the system has been based not on class or interest or ideology, but on the memory of the civil war. Important leaders in that conflict—many of whom served in 1916 too—only passed out of public life in the last ten years, and with them the enmities of the past. In the long struggle between the two groups, the antitreaty faction achieved the greatest electoral successes. They became not only the heroes of

1916 but the builders of modern Ireland, despite their rejection of the new state in 1922 and their responsibility for the civil war. De Valera, for example, served as prime minister from 1932 to 1948, 1951 to 1954, and 1957 to 1959 and as president from 1959 until 1973.

De Valera's success was certainly due to his ability, but it might also have been due to the events of August 1922. In that month, both Arthur Griffith and Michael Collins, by then the elected leaders of the new Ireland, died. Griffith's death was from natural causes on August 12, but it was probably hastened by the pressures of the time. Collins was gunned down by antitreaty forces in an ambush just ten days later when he was touring his native County Cork. He was a young man—still two months short of his thirty-second birthday—yet he was an authentic hero who stood well above de Valera at that time in the eyes of his countrymen. He had associated himself with moderation and compromise, although he had predicted when he signed the treaty in London that this would cost him his life. His death, and that of Griffith, left a great void in Ireland. They were succeeded by men with impeccable republican credentials. William Cosgrave, who became the first prime minister of the Irish Free State when it was formally inaugurated in December 1922, had been condemned to death for his part in the 1916 Rising. His deputy, Kevin O'Higgins, had been imprisoned in 1918. But neither man had the reputation or the charisma of Michael Collins. Furthermore, O'Higgins, a young man of only thirty–five years, was assassinated in 1927. De Valera, on the other hand, survived and served to a venerable old age. He was able to fashion a very different image of himself and the civil war from what had existed at the time. He was able to redeem himself in the eyes of the majority of his countrymen, but his enemies could not forgive him.

10
The Effects
of the Rising

The Easter Rising of 1916 set in motion the forces which led to Irish independence in 1922. As we saw in Chapter Eight, it is not certain that this had to be the outcome of the Rising, but given the response of the United Kingdom and the circumstances of World War I, it is what actually happened. Independence should have been a joyful occasion: Ireland liberated at last from 750 years of domination from England. But the triumph was a hollow one. The Irish Free State celebrated its birth with a civil war fought between people who had very different notions concerning what had been achieved. The protreaty forces, anxious to avoid further bloodshed, accepted the Anglo–Irish treaty of December 1921 as the best that could be secured. But the antitreaty forces fought on against their own countrymen for the privilege of continuing the war against the United Kingdom. The two sides disagreed on the issue of continuing the war, but neither believed that the Anglo–Irish treaty was a good one for Ireland. Both sides were disappointed in 1921 and they might be disappointed today were they to take literally the promise of the Rising

THE UNFINISHED REVOLUTION—A GAELIC IRELAND

The men and women who staged the Easter Rising hoped for so much, as they needed to in order to justify a blood sacrifice. Pearse, for example, died for four things; an independent, republican, Gaelic, and united Ireland. Two of these have been achieved—independence in 1922 and republican status in 1949—but Ireland today is neither Gaelic nor united.

A Gaelic Ireland was particularly important to Pearse because he and his fellow Romantic Nationalists believed that the key to rediscovering the historic Irish nation lay in the Irish language, a form of Gaelic. Many of the leaders of the Rising—Pearse and de Valera, for example—had come into the nationalist movement by way of the Gaelic revival, and it is not an exaggeration to say that without the Gaelic League and the interest it mobilized there would have been no Easter Rising. Pearse himself believed in an Ireland which was "not free merely, but Gaelic as well; not Gaelic merely, but free as well."[1]

The 1922 Constitution of the Irish Free State recognized Irish as the national language, and it was made compulsory in schools, but more than fifty years later, English is still the primary language of instruction and communication in Ireland, even in Dail Eireann. There are books, magazines, newspapers, television and radio programs, and plays in Irish, but they serve a minority audience. There are a number of areas in the west of the country, collectively known as the Gaeltacht, where Irish is spoken as the native language. A great deal has been done to promote the economy of this region to discourage emigration into more prosperous areas, but it is threatened by the emigration of Irish speakers and the spread of bilingualism. The Gaeltacht occupies only six percent of the land area of Ireland and cannot be totally isolated from outside

[1] Patrick Pearse, *The Best of Pearse*, edited by Proinsias MacAonghusa and Liam Ó Réagáin (Cork, 1967). p. 133.

influences.

There is a flourishing indigenous culture in Ireland in music, dancing and sports, particularly, but it does not exclude English forms. There is a substantial Irish literature in the English language, for example, and Ireland is an important part of the English-speaking world. A successful Gaelic revival would threaten the country with cultural isolation, but this is unlikely to happen. Only draconian measures of compulsion which are unacceptable in a free society can reverse the tide of English.

The language issue can still arouse intense passions in Ireland but the proverbial man on the street is not agitated by the threat to Irish and certainly cannot be bothered to master it. The Gaelic revival played a critical role in the revolution and became the official policy of the new Ireland, but it was always the passion of a very few and has failed to win popular support. More Irishmen are disatisfied with the failure to win a united Ireland than they are with the failure to win a Gaelic Ireland.

THE UNFINISHED REVOLUTION—A UNITED IRELAND

The founding fathers of the new Irish state hoped for the peaceful unification of the country, but this was even less likely after independence than it had been in 1914. There are at least six reasons for this, all of which relate in some way to the Easter Rising and the values it represented.

First, what was seen from the North as the disloyalty of the Irish Nationalists during World War I had alienated still further the Unionists who had remained loyal to the United Kingdom. This alienation was exacerbated by Ireland's neutrality in World War II. Notwithstanding the threat to civilization posed by Hitler and Mussolini, de Valera and his government, with widespread popular support, refused to commit Ireland to the war until the country was united. Irish neutrality was relatively benevolent, it is true, but it was neutrality nonetheless and was followed by Ireland's refusal to join the North Atlantic Treaty Orgazination in the postwar period. These policies drove the ultraloyalists of Northern Ireland even closer to England than before.

Second, the violence of the Easter Rising, the war of independence, and the civil war frightened the North. The leaders who had emerged since 1916 were far more terrifying neighbors than John Redmond and the Constitutional Nationalists.

Third, the new Irish state was born of the Easter Rising, and its patriotism, its myths, and its civic values were those of the Rising and the revolutionary tradition. Its heros were the men and women who had defied the United Kingdom—Pearse, Connolly, Clarke, Casement, de Valera, Collins, and the rest. These names and the values they represented were absolutely antithetical to the values of Unionism—loyalty to the crown and the British Empire, for example. The two could no more mix than oil and water.

Fourth, an autonomous political system which the Unionists could dominate had been created in the North in 1921. which the Unionists could donimate. This will be considered in more detail later, but for the moment it should be noted that although the Northern Ireland Parliament was subordinate to the United Kingdom Parliament at Westminister, it had full control of its domestic affairs, including the police. Unionists believed that their interests had not been so well protected since the Act of Union in 1800 and they had no intention of surrendering these new powers.

Fifth, Irish Nationalists in the North and the South consistently denied the legitimacy of the Northern Ireland Parliament, and this strengthened the determination of the Unionists to resist unification. Republicans insisted that an Irish Republic had been proclaimed for the whole of Ireland in 1916, and although this fiction was officially abandoned for a while by the government of the Irish Free State at the insistence of the United Kingdom, it was revived in the Constitution of 1937. Article 2 declared, "The national territory consists of the whole island of Ireland . . . ." Article 3 recognized that the North was not yet reintegrated but Article 2 was a constant irritant to the North because it implied that unification would only come on the Nationalists' terms. Irish nationalists elected to the Northern Parliament refused to take their seats until 1925 and were always regarded as agents of the South. Sixth, the policies of the new state were antithetical to Unionism in two critical respects. The first concerned the Irish language and the second the Roman Catholic Church. Douglas Hyde, the Protestant founder of the Gaelic League and president of Ireland from 1938 to 1949, explained that he tried to keep the league out of politics because, "My ambition had always been to use the [Irish] language as a neutral field upon which all Irishmen might meet. . . ."[2] But this was terribly naive. Apart from a handful of Romantic Nationalists like himself, Irish Protestants had no interest in the Gaelic tradition, and formal adoption of Irish language policies by the Irish Free State did nothing to endear unification to the majority in Northern Ireland. As Garret FitzGerald argues in *Towards a New Ireland:*

> The new nationalism created by 1916 owed much of its strength — perhaps even its existence — to the language movement of the late nineteeth and early twentieth centuries. In seeking to repay this debt, and, indeed, in seeking to give concrete shape to the aspirations of the men of 1916 who had been trying to re-kindle what they felt to be a dying nationalism, those who inherited the mantle of the executed leaders did in fact create a new Ireland much more alien to the Northern Protestants than the kind of Ireland that had existed before the Great War. . . . 1916 today stands as a psychological barrier between Protestant Ulster and the predominantly Catholic rest of Ireland. What to a majority of the Irish people has become sacred is to the Northern Protestant today an alien and even hateful tradition.[3]

Closely associated with the concept of a Gaelic Ireland is the concept of a Catholic Ireland. Unionists always feared that a Dublin parliament would be an instrument of Catholic oppression:

[2] Gareth W. Dunleavy, *Douglas Hyde* (Lewisburg, 1974), p. 38.
[3] Garret FitzGerald, *Towards a New Ireland* (Dublin, 1972), p. 12.

home rule meant Rome rule! Since independence, however, the Protestant minority in the South has been treated with great tolerance—in part, no doubt, because its small numbers and voluntary acceptance of the state posed no threat. The situation has been very different for the Catholic minority in the North. Anti–Catholic sentiment in Northern Ireland is produced by three things: a militant form of Protestantism, associated largely with the Presbyterian community; a fear of the Catholic majority in Ireland as a whole; and the traditional association between Catholicism and Irish Nationalism. Both parts of Ireland practice segregation by religion in their schools and churches, but in Northern Ireland this is compounded by segregation and often discrimination in housing and jobs, and in a level of hostility between the two communities which is totally lacking in the South. It has led to large–scale violence on dozens of occasions, including virtual warfare since 1969.

Freedom of religion is guaranteed in the North, but it has not led to toleration between the two communities. In the South, on the other hand, Catholics are unafraid of Protestants. Freedom of religion was guaranteed in both the 1922 and 1937 Constitutions, and Protestants have been secure in their worship, their jobs and even in public life. For example, Douglas Hyde was president of Ireland from 1938 to 1949 and another Protestant, Erskine Childers, whose antitreaty father was executed by the Irish Free State in 1922, was president from 1973 to 1974.

There is, then, religious toleration in the Irish Republic, but it is nonetheless a Catholic country, and the evidence of this is enough to convict it of sectarianism in Unionist eyes. Article 44.1.2 of the 1937 Constitution, for example, recognized the special position of the Roman Catholic Church as guardian of the faith of the Irish majority. This was removed from the Constitution by a referendum in 1972, after it was realized that it impeded discussions of Irish unification by implying that Protestant churches would have an inferior status in a united Ireland. This was a symbolically important act, although the article had simply recognized the social fact of a Catholic majority. But Article 41.3.2 of the Constitution goes further in that it actually endorses Catholic doctrine by forbidding divorce. Furthermore, outside the framework of the Constitution, there are other indications that public policy has been influenced by Catholic values. For example, the sale of contraceptives is banned. There has also been a particularly harsh censorship of books since 1929, which has resulted in Ireland banning an astonishing number of the world's greatest writers—Erskine Caldwell, William Faulkner, André Gide, Graham Green, Ernest Hemingway, Aldous Huxley, D. H. Lawrence, Thomas Mann, Marcel Proust, Bernard Shaw, Dylan Thomas, H. G. Wells, Tennessee Williams, and many, many more. Censorship is not an exclusively Catholic phenomenon, and Ireland was actually continuing a British tradition. But the Church has certainly inhibited the recognition of changing literary and moral standards so that, despite changes in the law in 1967, Ireland is still intolerant in this respect.

Ireland is, then, a Catholic country, but the relationship between the Roman Catholic Church and public policy has often been distorted in the North. There are very few examples of the Church issuing directives to the Irish government. One ancient case, when the government yielded to Church pressure in 1951 and abandoned a scheme to provide free medical care to mothers and children, is so frequently cited as the best example that we can be sure it does not happen very often. But looking for Church intervention really misses the point. The great majority of the founding fathers and Irish politicians have been devout Catholics. They have legislated as Catholics because that is what they are and not because the Church directs them. This is a fact of life in the Irish Republic, but it is inadequately appreciated there. Amendments to the Constitution cannot change the fact that Unionists believe a united Ireland would continue to be a Catholic Ireland.

It is clear that both Gaelic and Catholic values have been endorsed by the new Irish state since independence in 1922, and in this it has been true to the goals of the Easter Rising. But governments in the South, and their supporters in the North, have never ceased to claim sovereignty over the whole island. This has certainly contributed to poor relations between the two parts of the country, and as Professor J. C. Beckett has written from a Unionist persepctive, "to demand territorial unity while emphasizing cultural division was an irresponsibly dangerous policy." [4] It appears that this policy was innocent in that there was no deliberate campaign to obliterate the religion or the culture of the Protestants, only a desire to legislate certain fundamental Nationalist and Catholic values. But it demonstrates an insensitivity to the special character, and fears, of the Protestant Irish.

THE UNFINISHED REVOLUTION–A SOCIALIST IRELAND

Pearse's vision of a Gaelic Ireland was unfulfilled, but so too was James Connolly's dream of a Socialist Ireland. Connolly's basic beliefs were not those of his revolutionary colleagues, and although the Proclamation of the Irish Republic made references to equality and to "the right of the people of Ireland to the ownership of Ireland," these could be interpreted in nonsocialist terms. Furthermore, the first session of Dail Eireann endorsed a "Democratic Program" which was radical in its day but certainly not Socialist. It supported trade unions and the principle of public ownership of parts of the economy, and it guaranteed that "no child shall suffer hunger or cold from lack of food, clothing or shelter," but it was principally a platform for the welfare state and the mixed economy which Ireland has become.[5]

With the major exception of Connolly, the leaders of the Easter Rising and Sinn Fein were bourgeoise or middle class rather than proletarian or Socialist. When the Irish Labor Party, representing the Irish working class, decided not to run candidates against Sinn

[4] J. C. Beckett, *The Anglo–Irish Tradition* (London, 1976), p. 151.
[5] Brian Farrel, *The Founding of Dail Eireann* (Dublin, 1971). p. 87, and Patrick Lynch, "The Social Revolution that Never Was," in Desmond Williams, ed., *The Irish Struggle, 1916–1926* (London, 1966), pp. 45–47.

Fein in the general elections of 1918 and 1921 for fear of weakening the Nationalist vote, it permanently damaged its future in Ireland. The party finally decided to contest the first Irish Free State election in 1922 only to find that it was fought on the fundamental issue of the Anglo-Irish treaty. Labor was, therefore, squeezed out in the bitter struggle between the pro and antitreaty factions. These became the two major parties in post independence Ireland and in place of the politics of class, which would have worked to the advantage of Labor, the politics of the treaty continued to dominate Irish public life for many years. The Labor Party has never been able to substantially increase the seventeen seats it won in 1922. It has opted for democratic politics and continues to represent its version of Connolly's message to the electorate and Dail Eireann. But there are members of the I.R.A. in Northern Ireland today who claim to be The Connolly's true heirs. They are almost as hostile towards the bourgeois governments of the Irish Republic and the democratic Labor Party as they are towards the British. They continue to believe in the revolution and in their version of the workers' republic for which Connolly died.

CONSTITUTIONAL NATIONALISM
AND THE NEW IRELAND

In several respects, then, the Irish state has fallen short of the vision of those who gave their lives in 1916. But they were utopians. Mundane goals would not have inspired them to acts of heroism. Would they have died for what Ireland actually became? Recognizing the revolution as unfinished, however, ought not blind us to the achievements of the new Irish state. It is not Gaelic, united, or Socialist, but it is an independent, democratic republic. It survived the terrible days of the civil war without degenerating into military rule or a counterrevolutionary tyranny, as has happened so often in our time, and it has always had the support of a large majority of its people. Ireland is, indeed, a rare example, in this century of antiimperialism, of a stable and democratic new state. It is ironic that this achievement owes a great deal to the constitutional tradition which Sinn Fein had thought dead in 1918. There are a number of explanations for Ireland's success. Brian Farrell, for example, argues that because Ireland was already a modern society, the political upheaval from 1916 to 1923 was not accompanied by a destablizing social revolution that would have placed unbearable strains on the political system.[6] He also suggests that the Roman Catholic Church was a stabilizing influence. It had always endorsed constitutionalism against revolution and it threw its weight behind the new state in 1922—subject, of course, to the understanding reached with O'Connell and Parnell that it would control the education of Catholics.

Farrell further identifies two important political factors which have contributed to Ireland's successful transition to self–government. First, Dail Eireann absorbed the modern political forms and values of British politics. It did not have to search for a new model. In 1919, for example, it adopted the British system of cabinet government and parliamentary procedures modelled on those in use at Westminister. There already existed in Ireland a substantial consensus on the principles of representation and government and, Farrell writes, "There was never any serious dispute; a familiar and acceptable model—the Westminister model—was available and was simply taken over."[7] Second, and perhaps most important, Farrell argues that we should look at the Easter Rising not as a beginning but as an episode. It was, of course, an extraordinary symbol for the new Ireland, but we can best explain the stability of the new state if we recognize that the constitutional rather than the revolutionary agitation was the primary force in the Irish independence movement. It dominated nineteenth–century nationalism and reasserted itself in the Irish Free State after the brief revolutionary period from 1916 to 1922.

This argument is supported by the descriptions of constitutionalism presented earlier in this book—in Chapters Three, Four and

---

[6] Farrell, pp. xv–xx.
[7] Farrell, p. xviii.

Six—and is confirmed by studies of the transfer of power from the United Kingdom to the Irish Free State in 1922. Home rulers or Catholics were already in control of about half of the Irish administration by 1912 and, in an administrative sense, the home rule state was already in being, awaiting only the formal transfer of power from Westminister to Dublin, when it was blocked by the Unionists. Constitutional Nationalism had brought Ireland to this point and the effort was not wasted because many of the men who were ready to serve a home rule government in 1914 were still in Ireland eight years later. Lawrence McBride describes their response to the new state:

> When given the choice, in 1922, of either serving the Irish Free State, which was to be established in Southern Ireland, or the Unionist government, which was already established in Northeast Ulster, the overwhelming majority (at least 80%) of the highest ranking judicial and civil service officials chose to serve in the South. Most of these officials were the same men who had been willing to serve under the more moderate Nationalists in 1914.[8]

In this respect, the Irish Free State owed more to Redmond and to the patient work of the Irish party than to the martyrs of 1916 although F. X. Martin writes, "as if by an 'Official Secrecy Act,' no government since 1923 has been willing to acknowledge this fact."[9] Parnell was the last constitutionalist to be revered by the Irish. This is understandable, of course, because independent Ireland came to be governed by men who had rejected Constitutional Nationalism, but it is clear that constitutionalism was deeply ingrained in the Irish political system and in 1922, by overwhelmingly supporting the antitreaty faction, the Irish voters demonstrated that they too were influenced by the moderation of earlier years.

[8] Lawrence W. McBride, "The Transformation of the Irish Bureaucracy, 1892–1914," unpublished paper, 1978, p. 16.
[9] F. X. Martin, "1916—Myth, Fact, and Mystery," *Studia Hibernica* no. 7, 1967, p. 67.

THE EASTER RISING AND THE IRISH IMAGINATION

Constitutional Nationalism was revived in the political practices and the administration of the new Ireland, but Revolutionary Nationalism captured the Irish imagination. In part, this was because the revolutionaries came to power, and they had no interest in admitting John Redmond and his kind to the company of Irish revolutionary heroes—Tone, Emmet, Pearse, Connolly and the rest. The revolutionary tradition also captured the imagination of Irish writers who transmitted it to their readers. F. X. Martin believes that there was a deliberate theatrical element in the Rising which was, he says, "imaginatively planned with artistic vision. . . ."[10] He adds that it was also planned "with exceptional military incompetence," but this was of secondary importance. The purpose of the Rising was to stir the Irish nation with an extraordinary display of heroism, and in this it succeeded. As we saw in Chapter One, W. B. Yeats, for example, was captivated by the image, and within a week of the event, James Stephens was convinced that, "The blood of brave men had to sanctify such a consummation if the national imagination was to be stirred to the dreadful business which is the organizing of freedom."[11] No one was inspired by Constitutional Nationalism. But the theme of revolutionary violence, drawn from 1916 and supplemented by the war of independence and the civil war, attracted a host of distinguished writers—Yeats, Stephens, George Russell (AE), Daniel Corkery, Frank O'Connor, Seán O' Faoláin, Padraic Colum, and many more.

No one would deny the men of 1916 their place in the Irish imagination. Indeed, our discussion of the "unfinished revolution" and the role of Constitutional Nationalism in the new Ireland seems inadequate when we read Pearse's very moving poem, *The*

[10] Martin, p. 9.
[11] James Stephens, *The Insurrection in Dublin* (Dublin, 1966), p. 11.

Mother, which he composed for his own mother while awaiting execution:

> I do not grudge them: Lord, I do not grudge
> My two strong sons that I have seen go out
> To break their strength and die, they and a few,
> In bloody protest for a glorious thing.
> They shall be spoken of among their people,
> The generations shall remember them,
> And call them blessed;
> But I will speak their names to my own heart
> In the long nights;
> The little names that were familiar once
> Round my dead hearth.
> Lord, thou art hard on mothers:
> We suffer in their coming and their going;
> And tho' I grudge them not, I weary, weary
> Of the long sorrow—And yet I have my joy:
> My sons were faithful, and they fought.[12]

We should be moved by these words but we have to ask if the romantic view of violence in the struggle for Irish freedom, the "bloody protest for a glorious thing" which they represent, has been entirely beneficial. There is, in fact, a thin line to be drawn in Ireland between a legitimate respect for the heroism of the past and a cult of violence which bedevils the present. The latter can be seen in two different activities: the continuation of revolutionary violence by a small number of republicans, and the widespread use of the theme of patriotic violence in popular ballads and folklore. In both of these, the Easter Rising, the war of independence and the civil war are blended with Fenianism in a single image of patriotic sacrifice.

Revolutionary zealots continue to draw inspiration and justification from the nineteenth–century Fenian tradition and the even older tradition of agrarian secret societies. In his eulogy at the grave of O'Donovan Rossa in 1915, Pearse said of the English, "They think that they have foreseen everything, think that they

[12] Pearse, p. 192.

have provided against everything; but the fools, the fools, the fools!—they have left us our Fenian dead, and while Ireland holds these graves, Ireland unfree shall never be at peace."[13] For republican extremists, Ireland is still unfree and the Fenian dead now include those who fell in the struggles for the Irish Republic between 1916 and 1923. The I.R.A. campaign in Northern Ireland reflects this view, but it is a fundamentally undemocratic one.

In 1873 the I.R.B. Constitution was amended to read, "The I.R.B. shall await the decisions of the Irish Nation as expressed by a majority of the Irish people, as to the fit hour of inaugurating a war against England. . . ."[14] The rebels of 1916 never did wait for that decision. The Rising was the work of a tiny minority, "a minority of a minority of the minority," Martin calls them, recognizing that they did not yet speak for the Irish nation.[15] But their audacity was rewarded by their success. They soon won the support of a majority of their countrymen and inspired them to independence in 1922. Since that time, however, another minority has continued the struggle for the republican ideal. They rejected the Anglo–Irish treaty in 1921 and then rejected their own leader, de Valera, when he and most of his supporters came to terms with the Irish Free State in 1926. Each generation has produced new recruits to continue fighting and terrorizing both Protestant and Catholic Irish as well as the English. They claim to represent the republican ideal, but their vision is now a cloudy mixture of Revolutionary Marxism and Nationalism which even James Connolly would find unrecognizable. In more than half a century since 1922, they have been unable to win more than a handful of adherents to their cause, and the political wing of the I.R.A.—Sinn Fein—is now unable to win a single seat in Dail Eireann. Nevertheless, the terrorism continues, fuelled by spurious appeals to the republican

[13] Pearse, p. 134.
[14] Kevin B. Nowlan, "Tom Clarke, MacDermott, and the I.R.B.," in F. X. Martin, ed., *Leaders and Men of the Easter Rising: Dublin 1916* (Ithaca, N.Y., 1967), p. 110.
[15] Martin, "1916—Myth, Fact and Mystery," p. 108.

martyrs of the past.

Extremism is also fuelled by the celebration of violence in the Irish popular culture, particularly in ballads. In the 1920s, Sean O'Casey condemned this view and its gunmen in his plays at the Abbey Theatre in Dublin, but it survives. Men and women who would no more join the I.R.A. and fire a gun than rob a church are to be found in pubs and bars singing the glories of revolutionary gunmen. Their heros are as likely to have fought with the anti-treaty forces in 1923 or in the I.R.A. campaign in the North as in the Easter Rising. These events merge together in one rather bleary image. In a typical and extremely popular song, *The Patriot Game*, even de Valera is denounced as a traitor to the cause of the Irish Republic:

> This Ireland of mine has for long been half free,
> Six counties are under John Bull's tyranny.
> And still de Valera is greatly to blame
> For shirking his part in the patriot game.[16]

In part this celebration has an innocent explanation. The Irish have always loved to sing, and singers have to have something to sing about. Patriotism is a perennial theme but no one seems capable of writing a ballad about John Redmond and the Third Home Rule Bill, or about dominion status and the merits of the Anglo–Irish treaty. Rousing or plaintive songs of violence, be their subjects Wolfe Tone or the Cork Brigade in the civil war, win by default. But ballads, no matter how innocently sung, make bad history, and when they are not songs of Irish freedom but celebrations of the cult of minority revolutionary violence, they debase the events of the past and have an insidious effect on the present.

[16] Charles Carlton, ed., *Bigotry and Blood* (Chicago, 1977), p. 107.

WAS THE EASTER RISING NECESSARY?

This book has presented a rather reserved account of the place of the Easter Rising in Irish history. It was intended as a sober assessment and not as an exercise in extravagant praise or condemnation. There has already been far too much propaganda masquerading as history in Ireland, both North and South. We have seen, therefore, that although the Rising was the natural consequence of events which can be traced into the distant past, it was an anomaly. There were precedents in Irish history for revolutionary violence, but the dominant nationalist tradition in the years before World War I was constitutional not revolutionary. Constitutional Nationalism brought tangible benefits to Ireland before 1916 and was extremely important in stabilizing the Irish Free State after 1922, but its influence has been discounted in Ireland since the Rising and certainly in the popular imagination. We have also seen that the Rising was incomplete in several respects and that its effects have been mixed. In conclusion, then, we ought to ask, as others have asked, if the Rising was really necessary.

Conor Cruise O'Brien, the author of *States of Ireland* and a former Labor Party minister in the Irish Republic's government, has been the most prominent contemporary critic of the Easter Rising. He has stated unequivocally:

I believe that the political independence of a *26-county State* —which is what we have—could and would have been obtained peacefully on the basis of the Home Rule proposals reluctantly accepted by the Irish party in 1914. The subsequent armed struggle was waged not to bring our present 26–county State into being but to *avert* substantially that outcome, adumbrated in the proposals of 1914. This recourse to violence was a failure. It ended in the acceptance by a majority of the Dail and of the people of a settlement based in substance though not in form on Lloyd George's "Parliament of Southern Ireland" which in turn was essentially what was offered to Redmond in 1914. Subsequent improvements on the Treaty settlement were won by negotiation and could, obviously, have been won in the same way on the basis of the 1914 Home Rule proposals.[17]

In this statement, O'Brien uses four related propositions to prove that the Easter Rising and the war of independence were unnecessary. First, a partition plan had been "reluctantly accepted" by the Irish Party in 1914. Second, the Government of Ireland Act of 1920, which authorized two home rule parliaments in Ireland, represented essentially the same settlement for the South as the partition plan offered to Redmond and the Irish Party in 1914. Third, the Irish Free State settlement negotiated in the Anglo–Irish treaty of December 1921 and accepted by Dail Eireann in 1922 was "based in substance though not in form" on the terms offered to Southern Ireland in the Government of Ireland Act. Fourth, the subsequent improvements on the Irish Free State settlements were won by negotiation and could have been won, in the same way, by a home rule parliament established in 1914. The core of this argument is that the present twenty–six–county Ireland is substantially the same as the home rule state accepted by the Irish Party in 1914. Hence, the Easter Rising was unnecessary.

This is an intriguing line of reasoning, but, if we examine the four propositions, we will find all but the second open to question. First, the Irish Party had not accepted a partition plan in 1914. Redmond was willing to consider a temporary partition of Ireland but the Unionists would only consider a plan for permanent partition. As we saw in the conclusion of Chapter Six, the two sides were not as far apart as these positions suggest, but we do not know if Redmond could have convinced his party to accept any form of partition in 1914. O'Brien's second point is perfectly sound, however. The 1914 plan for home rule with permanent partition was, for the South, essentially the same as the southern home rule

---

[17] Cited in FitzGerald, p. 9. See also Conor Cruise O'Brien, *States of Ireland* (New York, 1972), p.89.

parliament authorized in the 1920 Government of Ireland Act, and rejected by Sinn Fein. But O'Brien's third point is wrong. It is not the case that the Irish Free State established in 1922 was "in substance though not in form" the same as the southern home rule state authorized in 1920, nor, by extension, "essentially" the same as the partitioned Ireland proposed in 1914. The Irish Free State was independent, and independence is more than a matter of form, it is a critical matter of substance. This, therefore, weakens O'Brien's fourth point, that a home rule parliament could have peacefully achieved the same improvements on the Anglo–Irish treaty which were won by the Irish Free State. While certain improvements—notably the abolition of the oath of allegiance in 1932, the new Constitution of 1937 and the declaration of the Irish Republic in 1949—were achieved peacefully, they were not negotiated. Only the redefinition of relations between all the dominions and the United Kingdom in the 1931 Statute of Westminster and the renunciation of naval rights in 1938 were negotiated. The rest were unilateral acts by an independent Irish government. A subordinate home rule Irish Parliament could have been abolished or overruled had it tried to act unilaterally. The critical point about the Irish Free State, then, was not its similarity to the home rule states proposed in 1914 and 1920—which was substantial—but its independence. And it owed that independence, as we have seen, not to peaceful negotiations but to the Easter Rising and the war of independence. Therefore, we cannot accept O'Brien's argument that the Rising was unnecessary.

It may be, however, that O'Brien's argument suffers by being too specific, and we might restate it in more general, and more speculative, terms as follows. Had home rule with partition been accepted by the Irish Party or imposed on the quarreling Nationalists and Unionists by the United Kingdom government in 1914, it is entirely possible that Southern Ireland would have become essentially what it is today by a process of evolution and negotiation. It would have had at least twenty–six counties, and probably two more, because partition would have been based on county option and there were twenty–eight with Catholic majorities. It would have been, as now, a stable democracy with strong roots in the constitutionalist tradition. It would not have been a Gaelic state, but it would have been strongly influenced by the Catholic and Gaelic traditions of the majority of its people. Finally, it might have become independent. As we saw in Chapter Six, home rule would not have provided a satisfactory relationship between the United Kingdom and Ireland, and there would have been a growing demand in Dublin for independence. Furthermore, with the northern Unionists permanently protected by partition, the United Kingdom might have been able to agree to independence.

Had World War I not intervened in 1914 to delay a settlement, home rule might soon have been accepted on these terms by the Irish party, or it might have been imposed on them by Asquith's government. As we saw in Chapter Six, the alternative was civil war. It might even have been imposed successfully as late as July 1916, soon after the Rising, when the plan was offered to the Irish Party by Lloyd George. Sinn Fein had not then emerged as the dominant force it later became, and the Irish Party had not yet been destroyed. But the opportunity was missed in 1914 and 1916 and was destroyed in the aftermath of the Rising. When the plan was finally attempted in the 1920 Government of Ireland Act, it was too late. Sinn Fein would have nothing to do with home rule.

A settlement of this kind in 1914 might have led to Irish independence, and it would certainly have avoided the great mistake made in the 1920 Government of Ireland Act, the creation of Northern Ireland. Home rule for the North was not seriously contemplated until 1919. Before that time it was assumed that a partitioned Northern Ireland would continue to be governed directly from Westminister. In 1921, however, two home rule parliaments were created under the terms of the Government of Ireland Act, one for the South in Dublin and one for the North at Stormont, just outside Belfast. Sinn Fein rejected the southern Parliament, but in June 1921, the men who had led the Unionists to the threshold of civil war to defeat home rule in 1914 found themselves in control of their own home rule state. Their original hostility towards the Catholic population was reinforced by the violent struggle for independence from 1916 to 1921 and by the civil war, which they feared would expand into the North. They therefore installed in Stormont a regime which regarded political power as a trust to be used to protect Protestantism and the Union from the Revolutionary Nationalism of the South and its supposed agents, the Catholic minority in the North. O'Brien describes what developed in the North as "an institutionalized caste system, with the superior caste—Protestants—in permanent and complete control of government, and systematically ensuring special privileges for its members in relation to local franchise, police, jobs and housing."[18] The southern regime quickly abandoned its revolutionary character as the Irish Free State reverted to constitutionalism. But the Unionists' attitude became a permanent fixture in Northern Ireland's politics until the United Kingdom government intervened to force reforms in 1969, following a Catholic–based civil rights campaign in the North. Even then the Unionists refused to voluntarily accept change, and it was their resistence, full of menace and sporadic violence, which enabled the I.R.A. to reappear in the North in the guise of saviors of the Catholic population. When the United Kingdom government belatedly dissolved the Stormont Parliament and established direct rule in March 1972, the Unionists had only themselves to blame.

Had partition been accepted or imposed in 1914, the Unionists would not have had the Northern Ireland political system to control to their own advantage. The region would have continued as an integral part of the United Kingdom, its sectarian politics diluted by the broader issues, parties and alignments of British politics. There would have been no Northern Ireland prime minister and no Parliament at Stormont to offer the trappings and illusions of sovereignty in an area more appropriately governed by a county council. Without Stormont, the Ulster Unionists could not have maintained the mental isolation which made them so resistant to

[18] O'Brien, p. 129.

change and the United Kingdom government could not have ignored the problems of the Catholic minority. Had partition been secured on these terms in 1914, Northern Ireland—which nearly went to war in 1914 against the prospect of Catholic domination—would not now be at war because of the effects of Protestant domination.

These speculations tell us what might have been, but they prove nothing because we cannot know that the United Kingdom would have conceded independence to a home rule Irish Parliament in Dublin. There also remains the tantalizing suspicion that the Irish people might have accepted home rule as a final settlement of the Irish problem, rather than demand independence. We must remember that the official policy of the Irish Party was to accept home rule as final.

What might have happened, therefore, had the Rising not occurred, is uncertain, but what did happen after the Rising is perfectly clear. In 1922 an independent Ireland, the Irish Free State, came into existence as the direct result of the events set in motion in 1916; events caused by the failure of the negotiations in 1914. It is ironic that the new state bore a very substantial resemblance in its area, its political institutions and its culture, to the home rule state which might have been established in 1914. But this should not tempt us to condemn the leaders of the Rising and the War of Independence for having risked so much for so little. They did not know that their struggle would be, in the end, for the Irish Free State becaused they aspired to a much more radical transformation of Ireland. Had their vision not inspired them to act, it is by no means certain that even the twenty–six county Irish Republic that we have today would have been achieved.

It is right, therefore, that the men and women of the Easter Rising should be revered as founders of the modern Irish Republic and their heroism be admired. But it is also right that patriotism should not be defined so narrowly that it excludes those whose commitment to constitutionalism and moderation contributed so much to the new Ireland.

BIBLIOGRAPHY

The books discussed below supply only an introduction to Irish history and the Easter Rising, but many of them contain bibliographies which will help the reader to explore topics in greater detail. With two exceptions, only books are listed, not journal articles, and the emphasis is on recent scholarship.

GENERAL SURVEYS OF IRISH HISTORY

Beginning students will find most useful Robert Kee, *The Green Flag* (New York, 1972), a lengthy but well–written book with a fine bibliography; R. Dudley Edwards, *A New History of Ireland* (Toronto, 1972); and several books by J. C. Beckett, the distinguished Belfast historian, *A Short History of Ireland* (London, 1973, 5th ed.), *The Making of Modern Ireland, 1603–1923* (New York, 1966), and *The Anglo–Irish Tradition* (Ithaca, NY, 1976), a fascinating defense of the Anglo–Irish. Partick O'Farrell, *Ireland's English Question* (New York, 1971) stresses the role of religion in Anglo–Irish relations since 1534, and A. T. Q. Stewart, *The Narrow Ground: Aspects of Ulster, 1609–1969* (Salem, NH, 1977) is a survey of the North by an Ulster historian.

A welcome new series for the general reader is the Gill *History of Ireland*, edited by James Lydon and Margaret MacCurtain, published in Dublin by Gill and MacMillian, Ltd. It consists of eleven short volumes by Irish historians: Gearóid MacNiocaill, *Ireland Before the Vikings* (1972); Donncha Ó Corráin, *Ireland Before the Normans* (1972); Michael Dolley, *Anglo-Norman Ireland* (1972); Kenneth Nicholls, *Gaelic and Gaelicised Ireland in the Middle-Ages* (1972); John Watt, *The Church in Medieval Ireland* (1972); James Lydon, *Ireland in the Later Middle Ages* (1972); Margaret MacCurtain, *Tudor and Stuart Ireland* (1972); Edith Johnston, *Ireland in the Eighteenth Century* (1974); Gearóid Ó Tuathaigh, *Ireland Before the Famine, 1798–1848* (1972); Joseph Lee, *The Modernization of Irish Society* (1973); and John A. Murphy, *Ireland in the Twentieth Century* (1975).

IRELAND BEFORE THE UNION

The Elizabethan conquest and the destruction of the Hiberno-Norman way of life is the subject of R. Dudley Edwards, *Ireland in the Age of the Tudors* (New York, 1977). Aiden Clarke, *The Old English in Ireland, 1625–1642* (Ithaca, NY, 1966), H. F. Kearney, *Stafford* in Ireland (Manchester, 1959), and Edward MacLysaght, *Irish Life in the Seventeenth Century* (New York, 1970, W 1950), consider Ireland under the Stuarts. The classic work on the eighteenth century remains W. E. H. Lecky, *History of Ireland* (abridged ed. by L. P. Curtis, Jr., Chicago, 1972), first published in 1892.

More recent studies include R. B. MacDowell, *Irish Public Opinion, 1750–1800* (Westport, CT, 1975, W 1944); Maureen Wall, *The Penal Laws, 1691–1760* (Dundalk, 1967, 2nd ed.), an important work which qualifies the popular view of the severity of Penal Laws; and Maurice R. O'Connell, *Irish Politics and Social Conflict in the Age of the American Revolution* (Westport, CT, 1976, W 1965), which describes the relationship between revolutionary America and Ireland. G. C. Bolton, *The Passing of the Act of Union* (London, 1966) is the most authoritative account of the creation of the Union.

SURVEYS OF THE PERIOD FROM THE UNION TO THE PRESENT

The most comprehensive survey of the modern period is F. S. L. Lyons, *Ireland Since the Famine* (London, 1973, 2nd rev. ed.), a balanced treatment by the leading historian of Irish Nationalism. Two excellent surveys which incorporate much modern scholarship are by Americans: Thomas Hachey, *Britain and Irish Separatism: From the Fenians to the Free State, 1867-1922* (Chicago, 1977), and Lawrence McCaffrey, *Ireland: From Colony to Nation State* (Englewood Cliffs, NJ, 1978). George Dangerfield, *The Damnable Question* (Boston, 1976) is a provocative account of the years from 1800 to 1922 that underestimates the strength of the Unionists' opposition to Catholic Nationalism. Other surveys include Patrick O'Farrell, *England and Ireland Since 1800* (New York, 1975); Nicholas Mansergh, *The Irish Question, 1840-1921* (London, 1975, 3rd ed.), by a leading historian of the British Commonwealth and Ireland; and Oliver MacDonagh, *Ireland* (Englewood Cliffs, NJ, 1968), a superb essay on the long–term impact of the Act of Union.

SPECIAL TOPICS FROM THE PERIOD 1800 TO 1922
Constitutional Nationalism

Daniel O'Connell and his two great campaigns for Catholic emancipation and repeal are the subjects of a number of excellent studies, including James A. Reynolds, *The Catholic Emancipation Crisis in Ireland, 1823-1829* (Westport, CT, 1970, W 1954); Angus D. McIntyre, *The Liberator: Daniel O'Connell and the Irish Party, 1830-1847* (New York, 1965); Keven Nowlan, *The Politics of Repeal* (Westport, CT, 1975, W 1965); and Lawrence McCaffrey, *Daniel O'Connell and the Repeal Year* (Lexington, KY, 1966). McCaffery has also written one of the few books on

Isaac Butt, *Irish Federalism in the 1870s: A Study in Conservative Nationalism* (Philadelphia, 1962), which complements David Thornley, *Isaac Butt and Home Rule* (Westport, CT, 1976, W 1964). Parnell has belatedly received an authoritative biography, F. S. L. Lyons, *Charles Stewart Parnell* (New York, 1977), which augments an excellent book, Conor Cruise O'Brien, *Parnell and his Party, 1880–1890* (Oxford, 1957), and Michael Hurst's shorter essay *Parnell and Irish Nationalism* (Toronto, 1968). Parnell's impact on British politics is skillfully considered in Alan O'Day, *The English Face of Irish Nationalism: Parnellite Involvement in British Politics, 1880–1886* (Niagara Falls, NY, 1977). F. S. L. Lyons has also written a fine biography of one of Parnell's successors, *John Dillon* (Chicago, 1968), but John Redmond is a neglected figure. Denis Gwynn, *The Life of John Redmond* (Freeport, NY, 1971, W 1932) is a useful, but dated work. F. S. L. Lyons, *The Irish Parliamen-tary Party, 1890–1910* (Westport, CT, 1975, W 1951) is similarly useful but dated.

Revolutionary and Romantic Nationalism

The best study of nineteenth–century Romantic Nationalism is Malcolm Brown, *The Politics of Irish Literature: From Thomas Davis to W. B. Yeats* (Seattle, 1972), a fine blend of literary and historical analysis. Leon Ó'Broin has written two books which describe the Irish Revolutionary Brotherhood and the trans–Atlantic dimension of Fenianism, *Revolutionary Underground: The Story of the Irish Republican Brotherhood, 1858–1924* (Totowa, NJ, 1976), and *Fenian Fever: An Anglo–American Dilemma* (New York, 1971). The impact of Fenianism on Anglo–American relations is well treated in William D'Arcy, *The Fenian Movement in the United States* (New York, 1971, W 1947), and Brian Jenkins, *Fenians and Anglo–American Relations During Reconstruction* (Ithaca, NY, 1969). Good biographies of the Fenians include two by Desmond Ryan, *The Fenian Chief* (Coral Gables, FL, 1967), a study of James Stephens, and *The Phoenix Flame*

(London, 1937), a study of John Devoy, and one by Marcus Bourke, *John O'Leary: A Study in Irish Separatism* (Athens, GA, 1968, W 1967).

The Church in Ireland

Several excellent studies of the Catholic Church in modern Ireland have been published in recent years, beginning with E. R. Norman, *The Catholic Church and Ireland in the Age of Rebellion* (Ithaca, NY, 1965). Emmet Larkin has produced a most impressive body of work including *The Roman Catholic Church and the Creation of the Modern Irish State, 1876-1886* (Philadelphia, 1975), *The Roman Catholic Church and the Plan of Campaign in Ireland, 1886-1888* (Cork, 1978); and *The Roman Catholic Church in Ireland and the Fall of Parnell, 1888-1891* (Chapel Hill, NC, 1979); and a collection of his articles from the *American Historical Review* reprinted by Arno Press, *The Historical Dimensions of Irish Catholicism* (New York, 1976). David W. Miller has published a distinguished book, *Church, State and Nation in Ireland, 1898-1921* (Pittsburgh, 1973), and John Whyte of Belfast has brought the subject up to date with his excellent, *Church and State in Modern Ireland, 1923-1970* (New York, 1971). The Episcopal Church is the subject of Donald Akenson, *The Church of Ireland: Ecclesiastical Reform and Revolution, 1800-1885* (New Haven, 1971).

The Land Question

The land question, the central social issue of the nineteenth century, is the subject of important studies by James Donnelly, *Landlord and Tenant in Nineteenth Century Ireland* (Dublin, 1973), and *The Land and the People of Nineteenth Century Cork: The Rural Economy and the Land Question* (Boston, 1975), and by Barbara Lewis Solow, *The Land Question and the Irish Economy, 1870-1903* (Cambridge, MA, 1971).

The Great Famine

The most popular book on the Great Famine is an excellent work, Cecil Woodham–Smith, *The Great Hunger* (New York, 1963). A fine collection of essays has recently been republished, R. Dudley Edwards and T. Desmond Williams, eds., *The Great Famine* (New York, 1976, W 1957).

Irish Americans

Studies of the Irish in America suitable for general readers include William V. Shannon, *The American Irish* (New York, 1963), by the journalist and American ambassador to the Irish Republic; Andrew M. Greeley, *That Most Distressful Nation* (Chicago, 1972), an interesting sociological study which describes the contemporary success of Irish Americans; and Lawrence McCaffrey, *The Irish Diaspora in America* (Bloomington, IN, 1976). McCaffrey has also edited an important collection, *The Irish–Americans*, forty–two volumes of original and reprinted works published by the Arno Press in 1976.

Specialized works include Thomas N. Brown, *Irish–American Nationalism* (Philadelphia, 1966), a pioneering study of the distinctively American character of Irish–American Nationalism. There are several studies of the impact of the Irish question on Anglo–American relations, Jospeh O'Grady, *Irish–Americans and Anglo–American Relations, 1880–1888* (New York, 1976); Alan J. Ward, *Ireland and Anglo–American Relations, 1899–1921* (Toronto, 1969); and Francis M. Carroll, *American Opinion and the Irish Question, 1910–1923* (New York, 1978). The most widely read book on this subject, Charles C. Tansill, *America and the Fight for Irish Freedom, 1866–1922* (New York, 1957), is by far the worst.

Home Rule and the Rise of Unionism

Constitutional aspects of the three home rule bills are considered in Chapter two of Vernon Bogdanor, *Devolution* (New York, 1979), but the political controversy is best studied indirectly through biographies. These include studies of the Constitutional Nationalists mentioned earlier, together with J. L. Hammond, *Gladstone and the Irish Nation* (Westport, CT, 1974, W 1938); Roy Jenkins, *Asquith* (London, 1967); Robert Blake, *Unrepentent Tory* (New York, 1956, W 1955), a study of Bonar Law; Edward Marjoribanks and Ian Colvin, *The Life of Lord Carson* (London, 1932, 1934, 1936, 3 vols.); and Leon Ó Broin, *The Chief Secretary: Augustine Birrell and Ireland* (Hamden, CT, 1969). Conservative Unionism is the subject of an excellent study by L. P. Curtis, Jr., *Coercion and Conciliation in Ireland, 1880–1892* (Princeton, NJ, 1963). There have also been several excellent studies in recent years of the Unionists in Ireland, including David W. Miller, *Queen's Rebels: Ulster Loyalism in Historical Perspective* (New York, 1978); A. T. Q. Stewart, *The Ulster Crisis* (London, 1967), by a distinguished Ulster historian; and two books by Patrick Buckland, *Irish Unionism 1: The Anglo–Irish and the New Ireland, 1885–1922* (New York, 1973, W 1972), a study of Southern Unionists, and *Irish Unionism 2: Ulster Unionism and the Origins of Northern Ireland, 1886–1922* (New York, 1973), a companion study of Northern Unionists.

THE EASTER RISING, 1916

The best introduction to the men and women of the Easter Rising is a collection of radio talks, F. X. Martin, ed., *Leaders and Men of the Easter Rising, Dublin, 1916* (Ithaca, NY, 1967). C. Desmond Greaves, *The Life and Times of James Connolly* (New York, 1971, W 1961) is an excellent biography of the Irish labor leader by a Marxist historian. Connolly's predecessor is the subject of a fine, recently republished study, Emmet Larkin, *James Larkin: Irish Labour Leader, 1876–1947* (London, 1977, W 1965), and the labor movement as a whole is thoroughly surveyed in Arthur Mitchel, *Labour in Irish Politics, 1890–1930* (New York, 1974). Sinn Fein has been neglected but is considered in Padraic Colum, *Arthur Griffith* (Dublin, 1959) and Richard Davis, *Arthur Griffith and the Non-Violent Sinn Fein* (Dublin, 1974), a study of the organization before 1916. Douglas Hyde, a founder of the Gaelic League, which greatly influenced the thinking of the revolutionaries, is the subject of a brief study, Gareth Dunleavy, *Douglas Hyde* (Lewisburg, PA, 1974), and Eoin MacNeill, the ambivalent leader of the Irish Volunteers, is the subject of F. X. Martin and F. J. Byrne, eds., *The Scholar Revolutionary: Eoin MacNeill, 1867–1945, and the Making of the New Ireland* (New York, 1973). Eamon de Valera is the subject of many studies including an official biography, Lord Longford and Thomas P. O'Neill, *Eamon de Valera* (Boston, 1971, W 1970). Patrick Pearse is the subject of a most impressive new study, Ruth Dudley Edwards, *Patrick Pearse: The Triumph of Failure* (New York, 1978). Roger Casement's life has attracted many writers, some concerned primarily to debate the largely irrelevant issue of the homosexual "Black Diaries," but there are several dispassionate works, notably Brian Inglis, *Roger Casement* (New York, 1974, W 1973). Countess Markievicz is the subject of two comparatively recent major biographies, Jaqueline Van Voris, *Constance de Markievicz* (Old Westbury, NY, 1972, W 1967) and Ann Marreco, *The Rebel Countess* (Philadelphia, 1967).

Biographies aside, the events leading to Easter week have been considered extensively in recent years, spurred on by the fiftieth anniversary of the Rising in 1966. Professor F. X. Martin of University College, Dublin, has done an enormous amount to analyze these events in a judicious way. See in particular his two edited volumes, *The Irish Volunteers, 1913–1915* (Dublin 1963) and *The Howth Gun-Running, 1914* (Dublin, 1964); and two superb, long journal articles, "1916—Myth, Fact and Mystery," *Studia Hibernica* (Dublin, 1967) and "The 1916 Rising—A Coup d'Etat or a Bloody Protest?" *Studia Hibernica* (Dublin, 1968).

The events of Easter week themselves are recounted in a number of books, the most detailed of which is probably Max Caulfield, *The Easter Rebellion* (Westport, CT, 1975, W 1963), based in part on interviews with survivors. Other useful books include Charles Duff, *Six Days to Shake an Empire* (South Brunswick, NJ, 1967, W 1966); Roger McHugh, ed., *Dublin, 1916* (London 1976, new ed.); Owen Dudley Edwards and Fergus Pyle, eds., *The Easter Rising* (London, 1968); Desmond Ryan, *The Rising* (Dublin, 1966, 4th. ed.); and Redmond Fitzgerald, *Cry Blood, Cry Erin* (New York, 1966). James Stephens, *The Insurrection in Dublin* (Chicago, 1965) is a reprint of Stephens' eye–witness account of the Rising published within weeks of the event. Leon Ó Broin, *Dublin Castle and the 1916 Rising* (New York, 1971, rev. ed.) describes the Rising from the perspective of the British adminstration in Dublin.

THE CREATION OF AN INDEPENDENT IRELAND, 1916-1922

Two useful introductions to the final years leading to Irish independence are T. Desmond Williams, ed., *The Irish Struggle, 1916-1926* (London, 1966), a collection of radio talks; and Edgar Holt, *Protest in Arms: The Irish Troubles, 1916-1923* (New York, 1961, W 1960). Dorothy Macardle, *The Irish Republic* (New York, 1965) is a voluminous account of the period from an antitreaty republican's perspective. Denis Gwynn, *The History of Partition, 1912-1925* (Dublin, 1950) begins with Asquith's Home Rule Bill of 1912 in a work which favors the Constitutional Nationalists. The abortive attempt to solve the Irish problem at a conference of the Irish themselves is thoroughly covered in R. B. MacDowell, *The Irish Convention, 1917-1918* (London, 1970).

The English perspective on this period is described in D. G.

Boyce, *Englishmen and Irish Troubles* (Cambridge, MA, 1972), a study of English opinion, 1918 to 1922; and Charles Townshend, *The British Campaign in Ireland, 1919-1921* (New York, 1975), a fine study drawn primarily from British military records. The Irish conduct of the war of independence is graphically described in several biographies of Michael Collins, particularly Rex Taylor, *Michael Collins* (London, 1970). The leading study of the negotiations which led to the Anglo–Irish treaty of 1921 remains Lord Longford, *Peace by Ordeal* (London, 1972, rev. ed.) The first years of the Irish Free State are considered in a scholarly new book, Joseph M. Curran, *The Birth of the Irish Free State, 1921-1923* (University, AL, 1980).

Two very interesting books deal specifically with the constitutional and parliamentary traditions in Irish history and their influence on politics in independent Ireland, a subject neglected in post–independence histories which have stressed the revolutionary tradition. They are Brian Farrell, *The Founding of Dail Eireann: Parliament and Nation Building* (Dublin, 1971), and Brian Farrell, ed., *The Irish Parliamentary Tradition* (New York, 1973). This theme is also introduced in a far–ranging and very personal account of modern Ireland: Conor Cruise O'Brien, *States of Ireland* (New York, 1972). The role of the I.R.A. and its influence in post–independence Ireland is considered in two well–researched books: J. Bowyer Bell, *The Secret Army: The I.R.A., 1916-1974* (Cambridge, MA, 1970), and T. P. Coogan, *The I.R.A.* (London, 1970).

INDEX

173